COMPLETE GUIDE TO THE

NATIONAL
PARKS

CENTENNIAL BOOKS

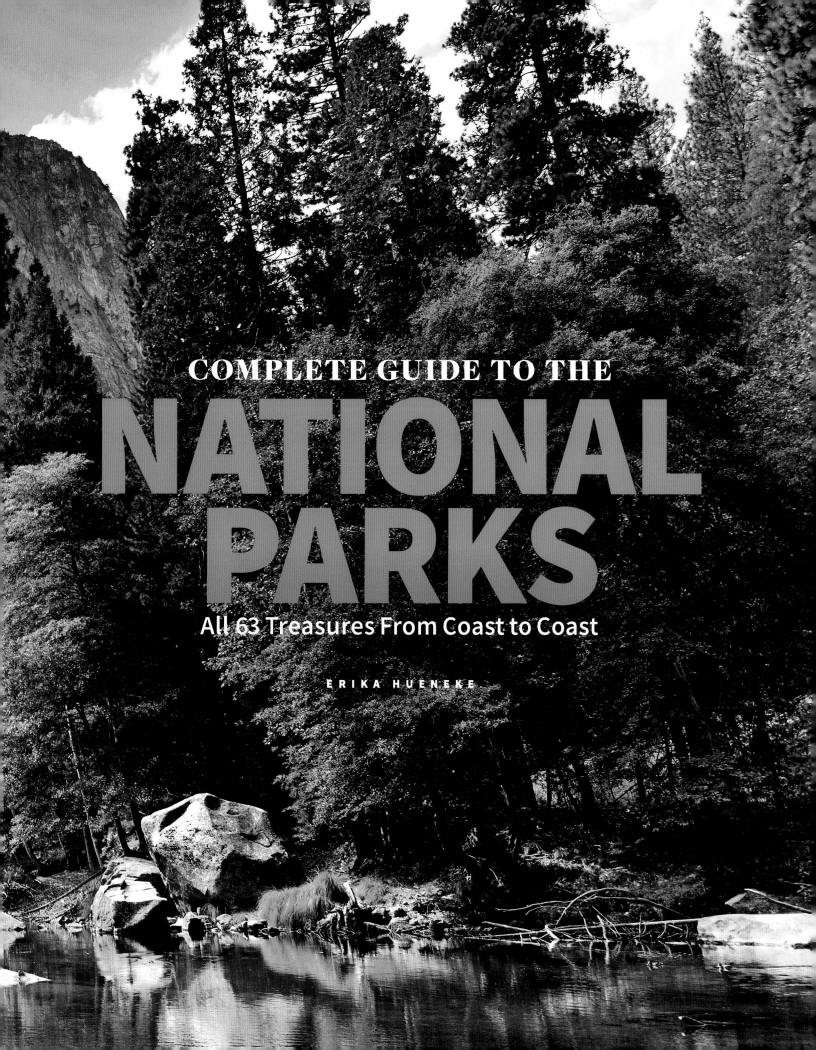

COMPLETE GUIDE TO THE
NATIONAL PARKS

All 63 Treasures From Coast to Coast

ERIKA HUENEKE

1
CHAPTER

PACIFIC NORTHWEST

2
CHAPTER

THE WEST

3
CHAPTER

CALIFORNIA

Sea to Shining Sea

HOW DO YOU summarize America in 192 pages? With almost 250 years of history and 2.8 million square miles of land, the U.S. isn't one story, but an entire anthology.

We believe the best place to start is the National Park System (NPS), comprising 400-plus areas of national significance, including 63 national parks—the crown jewel of the NPS.

Some parks even predate the creation of the NPS. In 1864, Yosemite became the first land preserved by the U.S. government, and eight years later, Yellowstone was established as the first official national park. As more and more federal lands were set aside, the need for centralized governmental oversight became apparent, and the NPS was born in 1916. Since then, the concept has inspired more than 100 other countries to create their own national parks and preserves.

Though these wondrous destinations are protected for "the enjoyment of future generations," they still face threats, from erosion and climate change to drilling and development. The time to see them is now —so tuck this guide under your arm and hit the road. You may just find you become a modern-day evangelist for "America's best idea."

Wild bison graze on the prairie in Wyoming's Grand Teton National Park.

1
PACIFIC NORTHWEST

Vast glaciers, arctic sand dunes, Technicolor
hot springs, deep blue lakes, fearsome
wildlife—all of these spectacles and more prevail
in this diverse corner of the country

WASHINGTON

North Cascades National Park

WASHINGTON IS NICKNAMED the Evergreen State, and nowhere is the color green on fuller display than in North Cascades National Park. Created in 1968, North Cascades boasts more plant species than any other national park—1,630 and counting. Its borders encompass eight types of forest, from ponderosa pine to mountain hemlock. Lichens and moss cover literally everything. Even the lakes are vivid shades of green.

Some 400 miles of hiking trails take visitors deep into the park's verdant environment—a place so enchanting that writer Jack Kerouac stayed for two months in 1956, working as a fire-tower watchman on Desolation Peak. He went on to write about the experience in his novels *The Dharma Bums* and *Desolation Angels*.

Despite its literary fame and location just a 2.5-hour drive from Seattle, North Cascades remains one of the least-visited parks in the NPS. Only one paved road—the North Cascades Scenic Byway—leads into the interior. The relatively few who travel it are rewarded with vistas of snowcapped summits, alpine meadows, pastoral rivers and more than 300 glaciers—the most in any national park outside of Alaska.

About 110 inches of precipitation fall on the park's western section each year—which leads to all this lushness and produces innumerable waterfalls. In this sylvan setting, the colors appear more intense, from Kerouac's "blue sunshine sky" and "sea of marshmallow clouds" to the majestic evergreens stretching up to meet them.

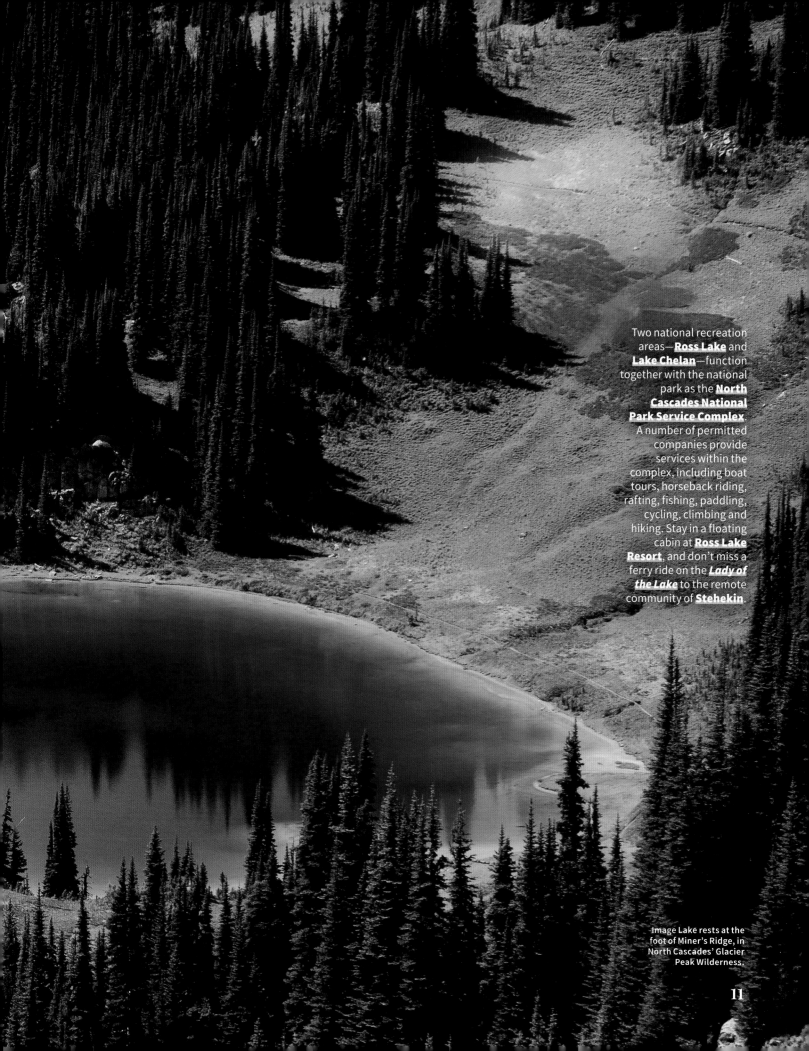

Two national recreation areas—**Ross Lake** and **Lake Chelan**—function together with the national park as the **North Cascades National Park Service Complex**. A number of permitted companies provide services within the complex, including boat tours, horseback riding, rafting, fishing, paddling, cycling, climbing and hiking. Stay in a floating cabin at **Ross Lake Resort**, and don't miss a ferry ride on the *Lady of the Lake* to the remote community of **Stehekin**.

Image Lake rests at the foot of Miner's Ridge, in North Cascades' Glacier Peak Wilderness.

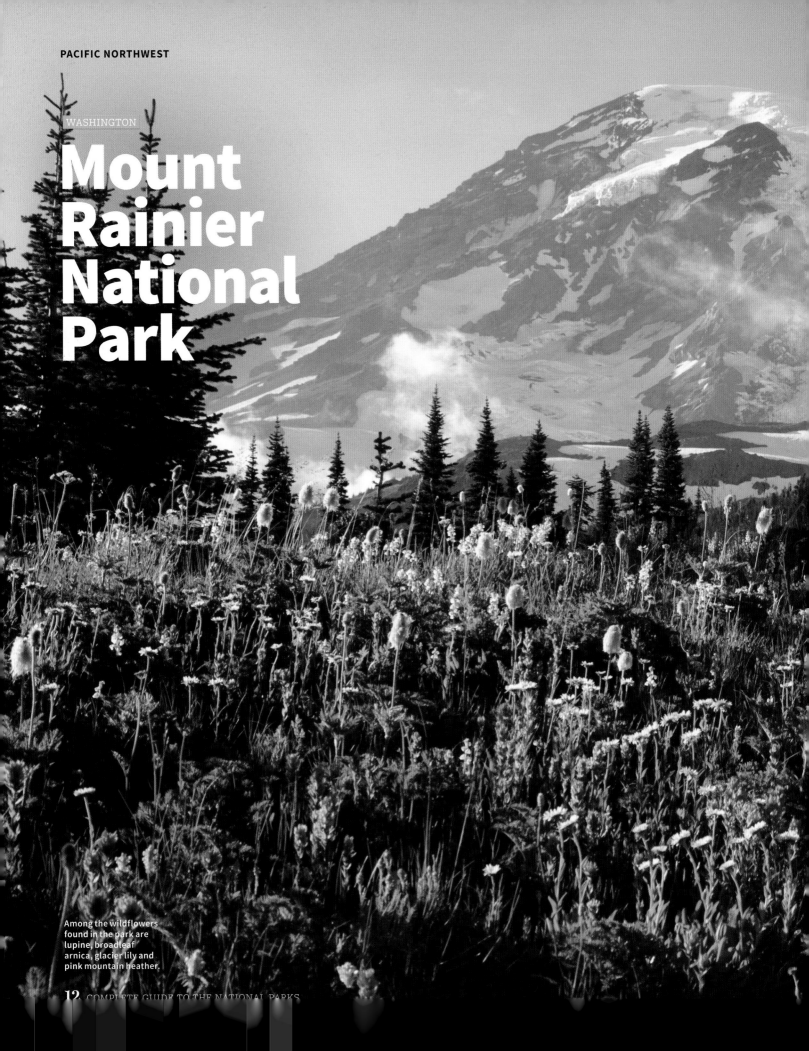

WASHINGTON

Mount Rainier National Park

Among the wildflowers
found in the park are
lupine, broadleaf
arnica, glacier lily and
pink mountain heather.

With five developed areas and three visitor centers, the vast expanse of the park quickly surrounds you. Make your way to **Carbon River**, named after the area's coal deposits, from State Route 165 to the pedestrian-only river trail — and look for the quarter mile **Rain Forest Nature Trail** or the 2.9-mile **Old Mine Trail,** which travels through deep forests to a mine entrance.

MOUNT RAINIER IS a world of contrasts: It rises 14,410 feet above sea level, but has five major rivers flowing from it. It's an active volcano, but it's also the most glaciated peak in the lower 48 states. It has ancient forests on its lower slopes, but fresh wildflowers in its subalpine areas.

In short, it's got something for everyone. So it's no surprise that the area has been used by the Native Americans for at least 9,000 years. Calling the mountain Takhoma, the Nisqually, Puyallup, Squaxin Island, Muckleshoot, Yakama and Cowlitz tribes all depended on its natural resources. In 1792, while surveying the Pacific Coast, the British Royal Navy's Captain George Vancouver found the area and named the peak after his friend, Rear Admiral Peter Rainier.

Today, the park is chock-full of activities, including train rides from the Mount Rainier Railroad and Logging Museum, gondola rides from Crystal Mountain Resort, 130 trails to hike, driving tours, foraging excursions—and even a wildlife park that hosts weddings.

WASHINGTON

Olympic National Park

There are 37 different species of fish living in the park's waters—fishing here is catch-and-release only.

While more than 20 roads lead into the park, the most frequented is **Port Angeles,** from the north shore of the peninsula, since it leads to the **Olympic National Park Visitor Center.** Drive west from the area and treat your eyes to **Lake Crescent,** where you can go for a swim, boat ride or hike on the **Spruce Railroad Trail.** And for a real treat, follow the side road from the western side of the lake to find the outdoor mineral pools at **Sol Duc Hot Springs.**

ALL EYES HAVE always been on the Olympic Peninsula, which sits to the west of Seattle and south of Victoria, Canada. After all, it's long been a source of some of the most diverse and coveted wood: Douglas fir, red cedar, Western hemlock and Sitka spruce.

In 1909, President Theodore Roosevelt set aside 615,000 acres as a National Monument, but loggers kept going after the region. Roosevelt needed to see it for himself, so on October 2, 1937, he visited the peninsula. When he saw what the logging industry was doing to the region he famously declared, "I hope the son-of-a-b*tch who is responsible for this is roasting in hell."

His harsh words worked. From then on, Roosevelt was fully committed to protecting the land, which became a national park in 1938 (signed by President Franklin Roosevelt) and now covers nearly a million acres.

The wilderness boasts multiple ecosystems and 70 miles of coastline. In the summer, boating, fishing, tidepooling and camping are popular, along with hiking (Hoh Valley is a must—you'll feel transported into a storybook land). For those looking to spot wildlife, Olympic marmots and mountain goats frequent the higher elevations, while Roosevelt Elks roam in the valleys and rain forests. Or just sit back and watch the night sky: With 95 percent of the park marked as wilderness, there's little ambient light so it's easy to spot the constellations. The winter months are popular for skiing, tubing and snowboarding from Hurricane Ridge, which sits more than 5,000 feet high.

OREGON

Crater Lake National Park

The park is open year-round, though some roads, trails and amenities close seasonally because of snow. Join a ranger for a guided ascent up **Watchman Peak** or a cruise around **Crater Lake**. Popular, easy hikes include **Plaikni Falls** (2 miles) and the **Pinnacles** (0.8 miles), as well as the 0.8-mile **Sun Notch** loop for views of the lake's **Phantom Ship island**. Prefer to drive? **Mount Scott** is the highest point in the state that you can access by car.

Sheer cliffs nearly 2,000 feet high surround Crater Lake, which is fed completely by rain and snow.

CRATER LAKE TAKES up less than 10 percent of its namesake park, but this cobalt landmark qualifies for world-wonder status: The deepest lake in the U.S., it's also considered the cleanest and clearest large body of water on the planet.

Long revered as sacred by the Klamath tribe of southern Oregon, the Gem of the Cascades has a violent past. Mount Mazama was once 12,000 feet tall, but a powerful volcanic eruption in 5700 B.C. caused its summit to collapse, forming a caldera 5 to 6 miles wide. Rainwater and snowmelt filled the crater, and over the centuries, life returned to its slopes. At present, the lake is 1,943 feet deep, and fauna such as deer, elk, bobcats, mountain lions, foxes, black bears, porcupines and bald eagles inhabit its surrounding old-growth forests.

Oregon's only national park was established in 1902, after conservationist William Gladstone Steel campaigned for its protection for 17 years. In 1909, Steel persuaded a Portland developer named Alfred Parkhurst to construct a lodge on the rim over Crater Lake, and the historic Crater Lake Lodge opened six years later.

Today, the lodge's back porch lends a spectacular panorama of the lake and Wizard Island, a smaller volcanic cone protruding from the water. Views also abound at the Sinnott Memorial Overlook, built in 1930, and on Rim Drive, a scenic 33-mile road that rings the lake.

Around the park, 90 miles of hiking trails ramble through soaring pine forests, blooming meadows and craggy peaks. Still, the greatest marvel is Crater Lake itself, so vividly blue that Native American myth maintains the mountain bluebird was gray before bathing in its waters.

At 1,943 feet deep, Crater Lake is the ninth-deepest lake in the world.

17

MONTANA

Glacier National Park

IN 1850, 150 GLACIERS covered what is now Glacier National Park. Now, about 25 are left—and visitors are flocking to see them while they still can. More than 3 million people entered the park in 2017, drawn as much by the retreating glaciers (which will likely be gone by 2030) as by the spectacular scenery of sawtoothed peaks, turquoise lakes, alpine streams, thick forests and meadows of wildflowers.

Established in 1910, Glacier is America's 10th national park—and one of its most pristine. Tourists originally arrived by train on the Great Northern Railway, whose president, Louis Hill, collaborated with influential naturalist George Bird Grinnell and other conservationists to create what Grinnell aptly nicknamed "the Crown of the Continent."

Built in Swiss chalet style, the railroad's Many Glacier Hotel is still operational on Swiftcurrent Lake today, and other historic buildings—Sperry Chalet, Granite Park Chalet and the Two Medicine Store—are also in use.

The park's other landmarks range from Lake McDonald Lodge, opened in 1914 on Glacier's largest lake, to the circa-1933 Going-to-the-Sun Road, a 50-mile highway that winds through nearly every kind of landscape in the park. But it is Glacier's wild natural beauty—700-plus lakes, 175 mountains and 71 species of mammals—that takes center stage. Even when the glaciers are a distant memory, these treasures will remain.

Shaped by erosion, geologic uplift and creeping ancient glaciers, the park covers more than 1 million acres.

More than 700 miles of hiking trails crisscross **Glacier National Park**. Get maps, info and more at one of three main visitor centers: **Apgar Visitor Center** near the town of **West Glacier**; **St. Mary Visitor Center** near the town of **St. Mary**; and **Logan Pass Visitor Center** in the middle of the park. At the latter, find trailheads for two of the most popular hikes: the **Highline** and **Hidden Lake** trails. See other wonders by classic wooden boat, courtesy of **Glacier Park Boat Company**, or by bus—the park's 33 vintage **Red Buses** make up the oldest touring fleet of vehicles on Earth.

Glacier National Park was inscribed as a UNESCO World Heritage site in 1995.

The park straddles the Continental Divide; when Pacific and Arctic air fronts meet there, the result is extreme temperature and weather changes.

WYOMING

Grand Teton National Park

"A beautiful piece of wild country in which people love to roam, and heart-lifting scenery," said naturalist Margaret Murie.

A 5-minute drive away from Grand Teton National Park is the **National Elk Refuge**, a winter habitat for the **Jackson Elk Herd**. When the elk shed their antlers, they are collected and sold at auction during **ElkFest,** which happens every year in May, the weekend before Memorial Day. Thousands of pounds of antlers are sold during this time, with the help of the local Jackson District Boy Scouts. Monies raised go to the **U.S. Fish and Wildlife Service** as well as to the local scout troops.

JUST 10 MILES south of Yellowstone, Grand Teton National Park is actually a combination of two National Parks. In 1929, President Calvin Coolidge, along with Congress, named the Teton Range and six lakes at the base of the mountains as a National Park. In 1943, President Franklin Delano Roosevelt created Jackson Hole National Monument, and in 1950, President Harry S. Truman united the two under the name Grand Teton National Park, expanding it to the current 310,000 acres.

Three million visitors explore the more than 1,000 plant species, 300 bird species, 60 mammal species—including bison, bears, moose and elk—and 22 kinds of rodents!

The diadem of the Teton range is Grand Teton, the 13,770-foot summit of the Teton Mountains, created by glaciers and eroded into shape by wind and water. A dozen small glaciers still remain in the snowcapped mountains, mostly in the Cathedral Group. One of the best views of the mountain range is from Jenny Lake, a popular fishing, swimming and boating location.

And for easy access, Grand Teton is also the only National Park with its own commercial airport: Jackson Hole Airport was built in the 1930s and became part of the park in 1943.

The Teton Range, which is 40 miles long, is the youngest part of the Rocky Mountains.

WYOMING, MONTANA & IDAHO

Yellowstone National Park

YELLOWSTONE'S CROWNING FEATURES—rainbow-colored hot springs, thundering waterfalls, ancient herds of roaming bison, powerful geysers spewing hundreds of feet into the air—sound like something out of a novel. In fact, when Yellowstone's earliest explorers recounted what they had witnessed, news magazines dismissed the reports as fiction.

Today, however, over 4 million annual visitors can attest to the marvelous reality of these geologic wonders, and Yellowstone endures as the largest and most diverse virgin landscape in the contiguous U.S.

Covering 2 million acres of northwest Wyoming as well as small portions of Montana and Idaho, Yellowstone was established in 1872 as the world's first national park—a "pleasuring-ground for the benefit and enjoyment of the people." Its borders contain more than 10,000 geysers, mud pots, steam vents and hot springs.

Of the park's 300-plus geysers, its most iconic—Old Faithful—erupts every 60 to 110 minutes and reaches an average height of 130 feet. Sightseers flock to view it in the Upper Geyser Basin, but other areas of the park are equally spectacular.

It takes at least several days to absorb it all—the Grand Canyon of the Yellowstone, 20 miles long and 1,200 feet deep in places; Lower Falls, twice the height of Niagara Falls; Mammoth Hot Springs' travertine terraces, sculpted by chalky white mineral deposits...the list goes on.

As America's oldest park, Yellowstone has faced challenges, from tourists feeding bears to ranchers poisoning wolves. Such practices have since been eliminated, and at present, Yellowstone holds its full original menagerie of large mammals. Lucky tourists can spy them still, including the oldest and largest bison herd in the country—though today's visitors know to keep their distance, as Yellowstone's most amazing attractions wield tremendous power.

Yellowstone
protects the greatest
concentration
of geothermal features
on the globe.

Microbes paint Grand
Prismatic Spring.

There are 67 species of mammals in Yellowstone—more than anywhere else in the lower 48 states.

During the summer, nine lodging options operate within park boundaries and 10 information centers serve visitors. To see the park by car, drive around the **Grand Loop**, a 140-mile figure eight that passes almost all the most famous sites. On foot, choose from more than 1,000 hiking trails. Or set sail on the water of **Yellowstone Lake**, the largest alpine lake in North America; guided scenic cruises depart from the **Bay Bridge Marina**.

Legendary Lodges

History and spectacular settings combine at these storied hotels

Jackson Lake Lodge

GRAND TETON NATIONAL PARK
One of eight lodging options inside the park, this 385-room landmark stands out for its modern-rustic design. John D. Rockefeller Jr. commissioned architect Gilbert Stanley Underwood (mastermind of the majestic Ahwahnee lodge in Yosemite) for the project, which was completed in 1955. Gape at the dramatic Teton Range through the lobby's 60-foot windows.

29

OREGON

Old Faithful Inn

YELLOWSTONE NATIONAL PARK

Take one step into the 76-foot-tall lobby of the 327-room Old Faithful Inn, and the immense grandeur and history of the most-requested lodging option in Yellowstone immediately envelop you. Even though it was completed in 1904, it still retains its spot as one of the largest log structures on the planet. Sitting across the way from the famous geyser, the summer lodge is open from early May through mid-November and has been a National Historic Landmark since 1987.

WYOMING

Crater Lake Lodge

CRATER LAKE

Perfectly placed in Rim Village with an idyllic view of both the lake and the striking surrounding volcanic cliffs, Crater Lake Lodge, which opened in 1915, has 71 rooms that lean into the serenity of the scenery by being free of phones and televisions. Enjoy your time away from technology by curling up by the lobby's two fireplaces, indulging in the Dining Room's sustainable local fare (highlights include smoked salmon and Dungeness crab) or going hiking, fishing or swimming in the lake.

WASHINGTON

Lake Crescent Lodge

OLYMPIC NATIONAL PARK

Built in 1915, this cozy hotel on the shores of Lake Crescent is a popular launchpad for adventures in the park's diverse ecosystems, from old-growth temperate rain forests and glacier-crowned mountains to 70-plus miles of rugged coastline. After a full day of exploration, relax by the stone fireplace in the antique-filled lobby.

Paradise Inn

MOUNT RAINIER NATIONAL PARK
Step back in time at one of the Great Lodges of the West. Annex guest rooms with private baths reopened in May 2019 after a full renovation; the season runs from May till late September. Its 121 historic rooms lack TVs and Wi-Fi, but no matter—you're there to hike 130-plus trails and admire the glaciated summit of 14,410-foot Mount Rainier.

The Canyon Overlook Trail's
crescendo is an unbeatable
view of Zion Canyon in Utah.

2

THE WEST

Be it the wistful painted deserts, the fanciful red-rock formations or the world-famous canyons, the American West has always had a particular pull, drawing explorers, prospectors and now, tourists

UTAH

Arches National Park

Meander through the labyrinth of narrow sandstone canyons at **Fiery Furnace**, which can only be explored on a ranger-led adventure. Book one at **Arches Visitor Center**, open year-round. Ideally, visit during spring or fall to avoid the blistering summer days and freezing winter nights. There are no lodges inside Arches. Reserve a spot at the 50-site **Devils Garden Campground** to experience the park by moonlight; book up to six months in advance. The town of **Moab** offers a full range of accommodations, restaurants and excursions (including to nearby **Canyonlands National Park**).

LIKE A SEUSSIAN SKYLINE jutting out of the high desert country of the Colorado Plateau, Arches National Park contains the greatest density of its namesake arches in the world. Visitors discover more than 2,000 of these natural formations, not to mention countless red spires, pinnacles, stone fins and giant balanced rocks, each uniquely shaped inside 120 square miles along the banks of the Colorado River.

Fine-grained entrada sandstone layered into perfectly parallel lines, combined with the area's slightly above-average rainfall and cold desert nights, allows these strange formations to exist. Ironically, however, the erosion that created these arches will eventually destroy them.

No one knows how much longer America will have these feats of nature, and the need to protect this vulnerable landscape was sparked in the 1950s, and nature writer and Arches park ranger Edward Abbey wrote passionately about it in *Desert Solitaire*: "Wilderness is not a luxury but a necessity of the human spirit, and as vital to our lives as water and good bread."

Established as a national park in 1971, Arches entertains with surreal skylines at every turn. Its 18-mile scenic drive lends panoramas such as Balanced Rock, right off the side of the road.

Explorers who get out of the car are rewarded with even more Kodak moments. Landscape Arch Hike leads to the longest arch in North America—a fragile ribbon of stone longer than a football field—while also passing Navajo Arch, Partition Arch, Pine Tree Arch and Tunnel Arch. Meanwhile, the iconic Delicate Arch (immortalized on Utah's license plate) might be the most famous image in a state bursting with legendary landmarks—a 3-mile strenuous hike (the park's most popular) takes trekkers to the foot of this sandstone bow.

From the Courthouse Towers to the Windows Section, not one inch of Arches disappoints. Dr. Seuss himself would be inspired.

Every natural arch illustrates 300 million years of patient erosion.

The North Window frames Turret Arch, encountered on the Windows Loop Trail.

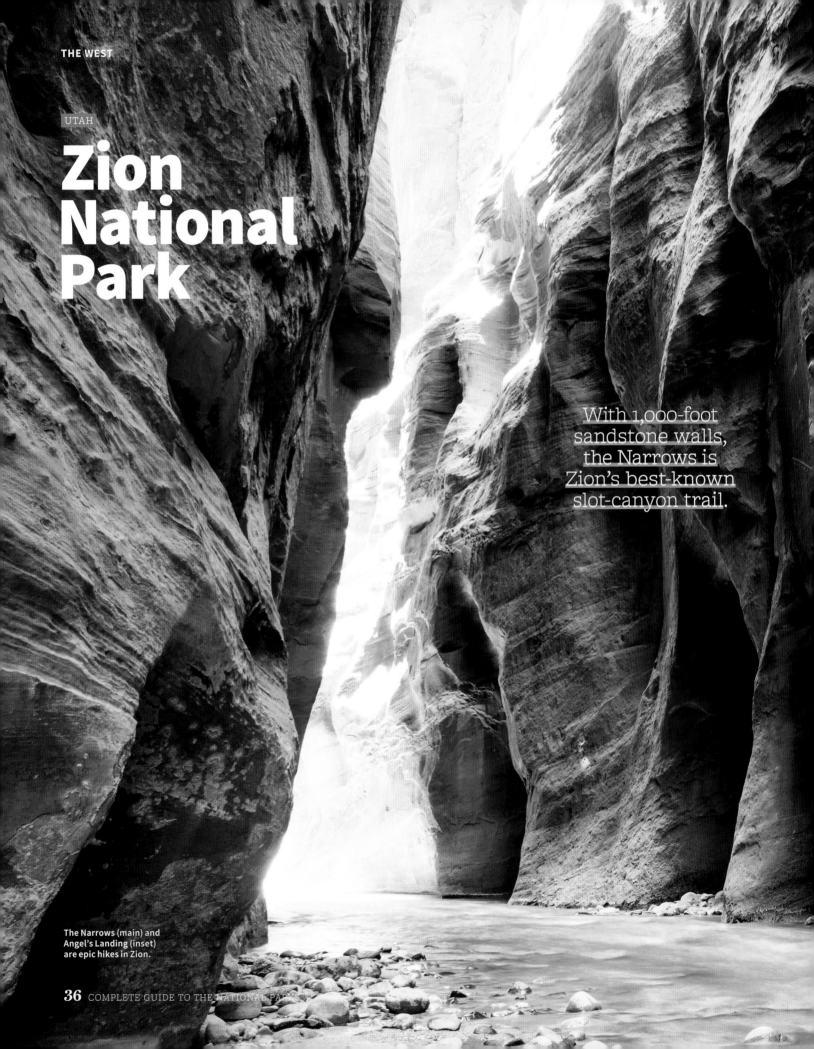

UTAH

Zion National Park

With 1,000-foot sandstone walls, the Narrows is Zion's best-known slot-canyon trail.

The Narrows (main) and Angel's Landing (inset) are epic hikes in Zion.

The south entrance is the hub of Zion. To sleep inside the park, reserve early for **Zion Lodge** and **Watchman Campground**, or try the first-come, first-served sites at the **South Campground**. Find numerous lodging and dining options in the gateway village of **Springdale**. If **The Narrows** is a must-do, avoid the early spring snowmelt, as the trail is only open during low-water levels. **Zion Outfitters** in Springdale rents all the hiking gear for The Narrows (waterproof boots and walking sticks are a necessity) as well as inflatable tubes for a **Virgin River** float. A free mandatory shuttle service maintains the serenity of the canyon during peak season (February to November). Shuttles depart every seven to 10 minutes from the **Zion Canyon Visitor Center**.

THE FIRST AND most popular of Utah's Mighty 5 national parks, Zion is also its most diverse. Lush green junipers and hanging emerald gardens contrast with ruddy-to-milky cliffs, carved over millennia by the Virgin River. An oasis in Utah's Southeastern desert, Zion's canyon walls surround visitors as the glacial river flows across the valley floor. The exposed rock layers reveal Earth's varied epochs, from swirling sandstone and ancient mudstone stamped with dinosaur tracks to petrified wood and marine fossils.

Instead of looking down on Zion's spectacular canyon from above, like in most famous parks, sightseers experience its Navajo sandstone giants up close, from the ground up. Nothing embodies this experience better than hiking The Narrows, which bends along—and often in—the slick-pebbled Virgin River bed.

Historically, apart from Native Americans, only determined Mormons traversed this remote and rugged landscape, with wagon trails for roads. It was these pioneers who named the area Zion, meaning "promised land." Established as a national park in 1919, Zion employed a Civilian Conservation Corps (CCC) team to carve out solid-rock tunnels and knife-edge roads such as the awe-inspiring Zion–Mount Carmel Highway.

Doable hikes such as Weeping Rock, Lower Emerald Pools and Upper Emerald Pool also offer great rewards, but Angel's Landing is the ultimate destination for bragging rights. Blazed by the CCC, this four-hour trek of switchbacks, thousand-foot drop-offs and a single chain handrail leads along a steep, narrow ridge to a 360-degree view of the park. It's one of the most hair-raising hiking trails in the entire nation—yet still only one of Zion's myriad marvels.

Bryce Canyon National Park

OPENING OUT OF a nondescript pinewood forest like a portal to an alien planet, Bryce Canyon has to be seen to be believed. In this 55-square-mile valley stand thousands of sun-baked turrets and bulbous columns, some reaching over 10 stories tall. This remote city of rock towers, called hoodoos, was carved by freezes and thaws over thousands of years.

Pursuing wayward livestock, a farmer named Ebenezer Bryce first wandered into the area in 1875, exclaiming this was "one hell of a place to lose a cow." Locals began calling his discovery "Bryce's Canyon," and rumors of its eccentricities made their way to Washington, D.C. Congress established it as Utah's second national park in 1928.

The park's 37-mile scenic drive skirts the rim, passing meadows dotted with prairie-dog colonies and accessing pull-offs like Yovimpa and Rainbow points, which reveal views of the entire spectacle from 9,000 feet. Four main overlooks command a vista of Bryce Amphitheater, the park's most popular area.

Early birds can explore the enchanted network of trails below the rim, diving deep among the glowing hoodoos on the canyon floor. The serpentine Navajo Trail to Queens Garden Hike gets explorers down into the heart of Bryce. Nearby, on the Queen's Garden Trail, trekkers can spot Thor's Hammer balancing to the northeast.

Whatever the path, each turn in Bryce Canyon brings visitors to yet another rusty giant with hidden passageways burrowing into the walls. Though not a secret—the park welcomes more than 2 million people a year—the otherworldliness of Bryce's beauty is still a discovery to those who step into its realm.

Shuttles run into the park from the **Bryce Canyon Visitor Center** from April to September, and most overlooks remain open through winter. **Bryce Canyon Lodge,** as well as **Sunset** and **North** campgrounds, provides accommodations inside the park during peak season, while **Bryce Canyon City** offers even more choices. At a high elevation, Bryce offers a reprieve from Utah's summer heat as the coolest of Utah's Mighty 5 parks. Late spring through early fall is ideal for hiking.

Bryce Canyon contains the densest collection of hoodoos (rock pillars) in the world.

A sunrise hot-air balloon adventure is an unforgettable way to see Bryce Canyon.

UTAH

Capitol Reef National Park

Get a close-up look at the natural formations by hiking in Capitol Reef. Trails for all levels are available—one of the most popular is at the **Hickman Natural Bridge**, a 2-mile walk that passes Fremont Culture ruins en route to the 133-foot rock bridge. The same trailhead also offers a 4.6-mile route to **Rim Overlook** and a 9.4-mile trip to **Navajo Knobs**. For a rim-top view, go for the **Boulder Top Trails**, with four trails of varying difficulty.

MOTHER NATURE IS showing her age: Capitol Reef National Park is in the Waterpocket Fold geology monolith, which basically means it's a wrinkle on the Earth!

But there's no doubt that she's showing more grace with each millennium, leaving behind stunning white domes (which provide the "Capitol" part of the park's name) and rocky cliffs (which the "Reef" part of the name honors).

The formations of these geological wonders took millions of years to cook up, with deposits from stones as old as 270 million years, uplift as high as thousands of feet, and erosion carefully engraving the stones into the majestic structures on display today.

For an overview of the park, head out on the 25-mile Capitol Reef Scenic Drive—plus three short side drives—which is one part surreally stunning scenery and another part adventure, particularly the Grand Wash, described as "a Disneyland ride in your own car."

Add to that adventure by truly embracing the Old West, camping out in a Conestoga wagon at Capitol Reef Resort. The six wagons, which can each sleep up to six people, offer the best in glamping, with new accommodations that have the luxury of private bathrooms.

The more adventurous can opt for canyoneering adventures along the sandstone cliffs through Get in the Wild, while families can bond over picking fruit in the appropriately named Fruita, a Mormon community with cherries, apricots, pears and apples, depending on the season.

UTAH

Canyonlands National Park

HOME OF THE iconic Mesa Arch, the Canyonlands National Park covers 527 square miles packed with canyons and buttes etched out by the Colorado River and its tributaries.

Tucked between the town of Moab and Arches National Park, the park is divided into four separate districts based on the rivers: Island in the Sky, The Needle, The Maze, and the Colorado and Green rivers. Historians believe that humans have been visiting the area for more than 10,000 years—art from hunter-gathers in Horseshoe Canyon is said to date to around 8000 B.C.

Ironically, when European explorers came through, they saw the area as a roadblock to their path between New Mexico and California. When Major John Wesley Powell explored the region in 1869, he described its predominant feature: "The landscape everywhere, away from the river, is of rock—cliffs of rock; plateaus of rock; terraces of rock; crags of rock —ten thousand strangely carved forms." It wasn't until 1964 that Canyonlands was established as a National Park by President Lyndon B. Johnson.

While cycling, backpacking, camping and rafting are all available within the park limits, there's no better way to soak in the natural marvels than by simply walking along one of the 74 miles of hiking trails featuring more than 50 species of mammals, from desert cottontails to kangaroo rats, and 273 species of birds (like the blue piñon jay) as well as a surprising amount of vegetation from piñon pine to desert plants.

For the best variety of hiking trails, head to **The Needles**, including the 0.6-mile **Cave Spring**, 0.6-mile **Pothole Point** and 2.4-mile **Slickrock Foot Trail**—or the longer 5.4-mile **Chesler Park Loop**. While driving along Highway 313 in the **Island in the Sky** region, keep an eye out for **Monitor and Merrimac Buttes**, which resemble Civil War ships; and in **The Needles**, look for the 50-foot-tall **Newspaper Rock** with petroglyphs.

The park was shaped by erosion, geologic uplift and creeping ancient glaciers.

ARIZONA

Petrified Forest National Park

On the park's north side, the **Painted Desert Visitor Center** is at Exit 311 off I-40. The complex features a gas station and a diner serving breakfast, lunch and grab-and-go options. The park is open year-round, but go in fall or spring for the mildest weather. Camping is the only way to overnight; nearby lodging can be found in the town of **Holbrook**.

The Petrified Forest welcomes an average of 645,000 visitors each year. It is the only national park containing a segment of Route 66.

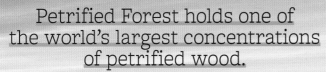
Petrified Forest holds one of the world's largest concentrations of petrified wood.

THOUGH NORTHEASTERN ARIZONA'S Petrified Forest was only established as a national park in 1962, this 200,000-acre landscape preserves millions of years of history. Here, archaeologists have unearthed Triassic-period fossils, as well as the world's largest collection of prehistoric petrified wood.

One of the original national monuments declared by Theodore Roosevelt in 1906, the park is comprised of two main areas. To the south, the park's namesake petrified wood dates back 225 million years and is made up of almost solid quartz. To the north, the Painted Desert is a fitting title for the orange- and pink-hued badlands made of clay and mudstone. In between sprawl more than 50,000 acres of designated wilderness. A 28-mile road winds through the varied scenes, with lookout points to take it all in.

Several hiking trails offer the chance to see the famed petrified wood. The Giant Logs route (less than a half mile) leads to Old Faithful, a fossilized log with a diameter of almost 10 feet. Another trail leads to Agate House, an eight-room pueblo home built from petrified wood between 1050 and 1300. Both trails can be accessed from the Rainbow Forest Museum.

In the Painted Desert, Kachina Point is the site of the Painted Desert Inn. Don't be fooled by the name, though: The adobe-style historic landmark now functions as a museum. If its walls could talk, they would tell of its 100-year history and its heyday in the 1940s as a respite for travelers along the historic Route 66 highway. But it would be merely a drop in the bucket compared to the millions of years preserved in the surrounding petrified forests.

ARIZONA

Saguaro National Park

Each side of the park has its own visitor center: **Red Hills Visitor Center** in Saguaro West and the more rustic **Visitor Center** in **Saguaro East**. In the latter, take the 8-mile **Cactus Forest Scenic Loop Drive** and stretch your legs on the **Desert Ecology Trail**. In **Saguaro West**, the **Bajada Scenic Drive** is a 6-mile loop with trailheads to day hikes like the paved **Desert Discovery Nature Trail**. To reach **Wasson Peak**, hike the **Kings Canyon Trail** (7 miles round-trip).

AROUND 1,500 PLANT species flourish in Saguaro National Park, but only one is king. The saguaro tree, nicknamed the "desert monarch," is the largest cactus in the United States, growing to 40 feet tall, living up to 200 years and weighing more than a ton at full height. Though the saguaro (pronounced *sah-wah-ro*) has become a symbol of the American West, it only grows in the Sonoran Desert of southern Arizona. Some 1.6 million saguaro trees pierce the skyline of Saguaro National Park, established in 1994.

In April, the cacti bloom with pretty white blossoms—Arizona's state flower. Wildflowers also put on a spring show: Photographers are in heaven amid a rainbow of brittlebushes, desert marigolds, globe mallows, lupines and Mexican poppies.

The best place to encounter Saguaro's signature cactus is the Tucson Mountain District, aka Saguaro West. Relatively hot and arid, this low desert is home to coyotes, desert tortoises, javelinas and quail, as well as 4,687-foot Wasson Peak.

To the east lies the Rincon Mountain District (Saguaro East), where the saguaro forest gives way to higher-elevation pine forests that support wildlife like black bears, deer and Mexican spotted owls. Between the two districts sits the city of Tucson.

Scenic drives, panoramic overlooks and 165 miles of hiking trails provide vantage points for observing the stately saguaros as they rule over the vibrant Sonoran— boasting the widest variety of life of any desert on the continent.

The saguaro cactus is a source of food and shelter for many desert animals.

ARIZONA

Grand Canyon National Park

AS GRAND AS THE STATISTICS

are—1.2 million acres, 277 miles long, 4,000 feet deep—nothing prepares the 5 million-plus annual visitors for the magnitude of Grand Canyon National Park. Our second-most–visited national park celebrated its 100th birthday in 2019 and still has many stories to tell.

The South Rim is the most popular destination and the gateway to iconic overlooks such as Yavapai and Mather points. More intrepid souls venture to the remote North Rim (closed in winter), where higher elevations mean unparalleled views like the ones from Point Imperial and the West Rim, where the glass-bottom Skywalk hovers 4,000 feet above the canyon floor.

Exploration here is hands-on and up-close. Riding a mule down into the canyon, biking along the rim, hiking trails like Kaibab or Grandview and rafting the Colorado River reveal the living history of this place. No matter the angle of the view, the word "grand" doesn't seem quite grand enough.

The Colorado River cut
the mile-deep Grand Canyon
over millions of years.

49

Most visitors coming from **Flagstaff** take Highway 180 North into the park, but entering through the lesser-used east entrance on **Highway 89 North** is a fun alternative. Stop at viewpoints overlooking the **Little Colorado River Gorge** and again at the **Desert View Watchtower**, built by famed architect Mary Colter in 1932. Summer and spring break see the most visitors, so if you plan to stay overnight in the park during these times, book at least a year in advance. Campers need a permit.

Scientists now believe the Grand Canyon began as a series of smaller canyons about 70 million years ago.

The Grand Canyon exhibits three of the four eras of geologic time.

NEVADA

Great Basin National Park

The 12-mile long **Wheeler Peak Scenic Drive** along the mountain road, starting at the park boundary at Nevada Highway 488, is a great introduction to the area, welcoming you in with sprawling views up through elevation changes of 4,000 feet to experience the peaks and deserts. At the end of the drive is the 0.4-mile **Sky Islands Forest Trail**, which invites you into the high alpine coniferous forest. Pack a picnic lunch and enjoy it at **Mather Outlook**, which features picturesque views of **Lehman Creek** drainage.

GREAT BASIN NATIONAL PARK

proudly brags about a rather unusual honor: It's one of the least-visited parks in the country. But with that comes the ability to explore the area—which houses Nevada's second highest peak—undisturbed, just the way Mother Nature intended it.

And this park is packed full of surprising delights around every corner. While there are at least 40 known caves divided into four regions (Lehman Hill Caves, Baker Creek Caves, Snake Creek Caves and Alpine Cave), the only one open to the public is the Lehman Caves. Sitting at about 7,000 feet, the cave is accessible on a guided tour (either the 60-minute Lodge Room Tour or 90-minute Grand Palace Tour, which includes a visit to the Parachute Shield cave formation). For a different take, stop by the Upper Pictograph Cave with cave art from the Fremont tribe which is believed to date back to 1300 B.C. to 1000 B.C.

If you prefer looking up the skies, Great Basin is a designated International Dark Sky Park—and when conditions are just right, the Andromeda Galaxy and the Milky Way can be spotted with the naked eye. The level of darkness here is so unparalleled that it's been referred to as an "endangered resource."

Also unique to the area, sitting near the region's only glacier, are the bristlecone pines—some of which are more than 3,000 years old. To put that in perspective, these trees have been there since King Tut was around!

The Great Basin ecosystem drains inward—no precipitation in the 200,000-square-mile region flows into the ocean

Carlsbad Caverns National Park

BENEATH THE SURFACE of the Chihuahuan Desert lies a hidden world—enormous stalactites and stalagmites, 18-foot gypsum "chandeliers" and the largest cave chamber in North America. Established as a national monument in 1923, then designated a national park in 1930, Carlsbad Caverns is a limestone labyrinth so outstanding that UNESCO inscribed it as a World Heritage site.

Thirty miles of mapped caves still intrigue researchers, while visitors can explore 3 miles of subterranean passageways. Formed as acidic groundwater slowly wore down limestone that was once part of an ancient undersea reef, Carlsbad Caverns is most famous for its aptly named Big Room. Self-guided tours (tickets required) lead travelers 750 feet down the steep Natural Entrance Trail into the 8.2-acre chamber with its many bizarre geologic features. Ranger-guided group tours delve into the park's more-adventurous restricted areas, such as King's Palace, Spider Cave and Hall of the White Giant.

Rivaling Carlsbad Caverns' grandeur is its seasonal exodus of Mexican free-tailed bats each night. The flight led to the discovery of the cave in the 1880s, and it remains one of its most amazing phenomena—which is saying a lot for a place that's been called "the Grand Canyon with a roof over it."

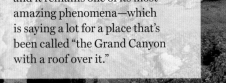

Some 119 caves have been recorded in Carlsbad Caverns.

Park rangers host a free **Bat Flight Program** on summer evenings at the outdoor amphitheater, near the mouth of the cave. The best flights take place in August and September. At the visitor center, **Carlsbad Caverns Trading Company** serves sandwiches, salads and snacks. As there is no overnight lodging or campground in the park, stay in **Carlsbad**, 20 miles away. Combine a visit to the caverns with a trip to **Guadalupe Mountains National Park**, 40 minutes away in Texas.

NEW MEXICO

White Sands National Park

A DESCRIPTION OF White Sands National Park reads like a personal ad: enjoys picnics, sunset strolls, moongazing and long walks in the sand. In fact, this rare gypsum dune field—the largest in the world—is so pretty that simply wandering around staring at it is the top activity.

Established as a national monument in 1933 and a national park in 2019, White Sands receives the most visitors of any NPS site in New Mexico. Day-trippers come to cruise down Dunes Drive (16 miles round-trip), which heads into the heart of the site from the visitor center, passing pull-offs, covered picnic spots and five trailheads. By day, visitors set up beach umbrellas and sled down the dunes; by night, they watch as light from the full moon reflects off the snow-white sand.

Located in the Tularosa Basin of the Chihuahuan Desert, the dune field formed as melting snow from the slopes of the surrounding mountains deposited gypsum into seasonal Lake Lucero. As the lake fills then evaporates each year, the dunes grow; they now range from 10 to 60 feet.

The dune field extends for 275 square miles, though only 115 square miles are protected within the monument; the remainder is on private military land. Look closely and you'll see it's not just humans who have taken to the unique habitat—more than 800 species of animals also call the park home, including fish, birds, frogs, foxes, coyotes and plenty of reptiles.

White Sands' dune field is very active, with some dunes shifting up to 30 feet a year.

Legend speaks of a ghost bride, La Pavura Blanca, who still searches for her lost lover among the dunes.

Start at the adobe visitor center, constructed in the 1930s in Spanish Pueblo style. Here you can buy cheap plastic sleds for a day of sledding on the dunes. Hiking trails include the **Interdune Boardwalk** (0.4-mile round-trip), **Dune Life Nature Trail** (1-mile loop) and the demanding **Alkali Flat Trail** (5 miles, no shade). Accommodations and amenities are available in the nearby towns of **Alamogordo** and **Las Cruces**. Note: Because White Sands adjoins White Sands Missile Range, the park occasionally closes during missile testing.

COLORADO

Great Sand Dunes National Park & Preserve

The park, including the **Visitor Center** and **Pinyon Flats Campground**, is at the north end of CO 150. Rent sandboards and sand sleds year-round from **Kristi Mountain Sports** in **Alamosa**. Hiking and horseback riding are popular pastimes; favorite trails include the **Montville Nature Trail** and **Mosca Pass**. Stay at the **Zapata Ranch** to book a horseback ride through **Zapata Partners**, the only park-authorized horseback-riding outfitter.

Outfitters provide
gear for sand sledding
and sandboarding
on the dunes.

IN A DISTINCTIVE corner of south-central Colorado, you don't need snow to sled. And you don't need an ocean to go to the beach. You do, however, need closed-toe shoes in the scalding sand.

This geographic curiosity is Great Sand Dunes National Park, designated in 2004 and home to the tallest sand dunes in North America. Covering more than 30 square miles between the San Juan Mountains and the Sangre de Cristo range, the dune field resulted when mountain streams deposited sand into prehistoric shallow lakes in the San Luis Valley and the lakes eventually dried up. Wind took over from there, sculpting the sand into towering mounds, some more than 700 feet high.

The highest, Star Dune, reaches 750 feet, and a round-trip hike to the summit requires five hours. Alternately, 699-foot High Dune, entailing a two-hour round-trip, is the most popular to explore. But with no designated trails in the sand, visitors are free to play wherever they wish.

Baking in the summer, the sand's surface can reach 150 degrees, but the dunes cool in the evenings and mornings. Visitors can seek refreshment at seasonal Medano Creek, which cuts an unlikely stream through the desertscape after the spring snowmelt. Nicknamed Colorado's secret beach, the area fills with families in late May and early June. From hot sand to cool creek, the park forges a lively playground for adults and kids alike.

Six types of dunes are found within Great Sand Dunes' 149,137 acres.

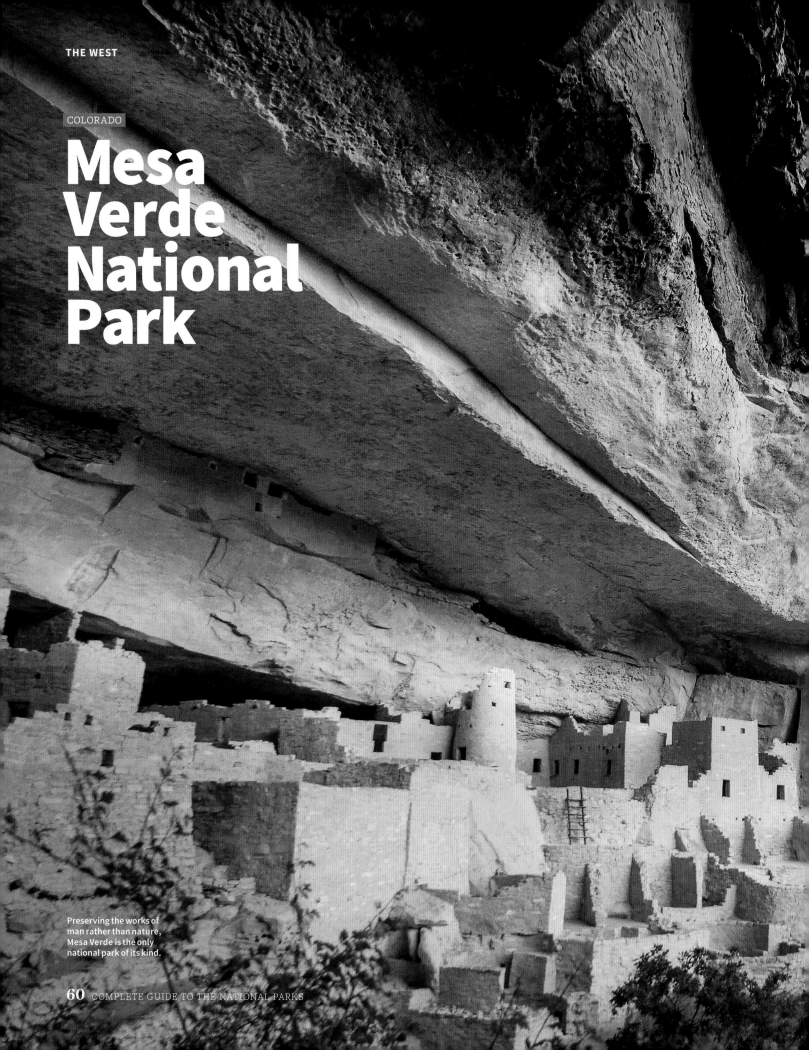

COLORADO

Mesa Verde National Park

Preserving the works of man rather than nature, Mesa Verde is the only national park of its kind.

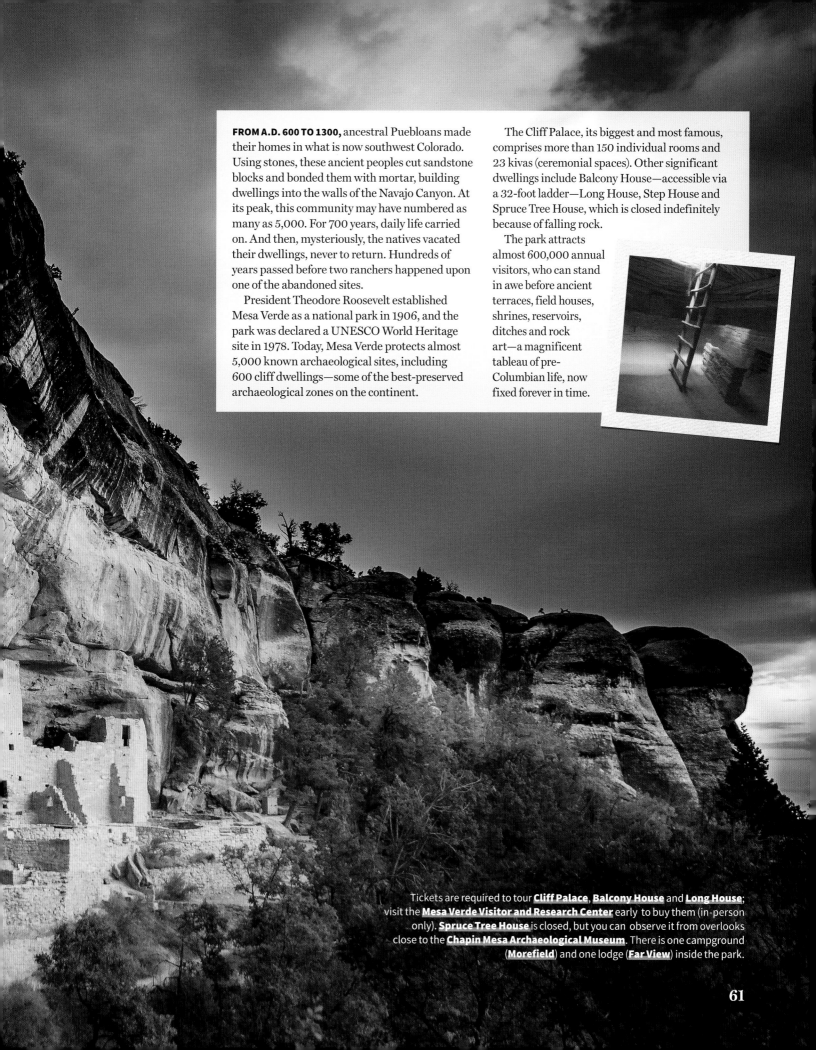

FROM A.D. 600 TO 1300, ancestral Puebloans made their homes in what is now southwest Colorado. Using stones, these ancient peoples cut sandstone blocks and bonded them with mortar, building dwellings into the walls of the Navajo Canyon. At its peak, this community may have numbered as many as 5,000. For 700 years, daily life carried on. And then, mysteriously, the natives vacated their dwellings, never to return. Hundreds of years passed before two ranchers happened upon one of the abandoned sites.

President Theodore Roosevelt established Mesa Verde as a national park in 1906, and the park was declared a UNESCO World Heritage site in 1978. Today, Mesa Verde protects almost 5,000 known archaeological sites, including 600 cliff dwellings—some of the best-preserved archaeological zones on the continent.

The Cliff Palace, its biggest and most famous, comprises more than 150 individual rooms and 23 kivas (ceremonial spaces). Other significant dwellings include Balcony House—accessible via a 32-foot ladder—Long House, Step House and Spruce Tree House, which is closed indefinitely because of falling rock.

The park attracts almost 600,000 annual visitors, who can stand in awe before ancient terraces, field houses, shrines, reservoirs, ditches and rock art—a magnificent tableau of pre-Columbian life, now fixed forever in time.

Tickets are required to tour **Cliff Palace**, **Balcony House** and **Long House**; visit the **Mesa Verde Visitor and Research Center** early to buy them (in-person only). **Spruce Tree House** is closed, but you can observe it from overlooks close to the **Chapin Mesa Archaeological Museum**. There is one campground (**Morefield**) and one lodge (**Far View**) inside the park.

COLORADO

Rocky Mountain National Park

IN THE UNITED STATES' 10th national park, a two-lane highway leads into the sky. Completed in 1932 and climbing to 12,183 feet, Trail Ridge Road is America's highest continuous paved highway. The road provides exceptional access to some of the nation's finest alpine country, connecting the park's eastern and western entrances and winding for 48 miles across forests, meadows, treeless tundra and the Continental Divide.

Elsewhere in the park, Bear Lake's flat, 0.6-mile nature trail is one of Rocky Mountain's most popular hikes. And Pike's Peak, though only the 31st-tallest summit in the Rockies, is the most-traversed mountain in all of North America.

For the park's 4.5 million annual visitors, these superlatives are only surpassed by Rocky Mountain's diverse animal populations. Wildlife viewing is the park's top attraction, thanks to the impressive playbill of "charismatic megafauna" such as elk, mule deer, moose and bighorn sheep. In total, 67 species of mammals call the park home, including marmots and pikas.

In 2015, the park turned 100 years old, and it owes its existence in part to naturalist, guide and local lodge owner Enos Mills, who advocated for its creation. His endeavor met with success when President Woodrow Wilson signed the park into law in 1915. Today, as one of the most actively explored national parks in the country, RMNP has solidified its standing as a prized national treasure.

There are 156 lakes in the park, but due to the cold water and a lack of spawning habitat, only 48 contain trout.

More than 100 peaks reach an elevation of at least 11,000 feet in Rocky Mountain National Park.

A 1.5-hour drive from **Denver**, the tourist town of **Estes Park** is the main gateway to the park. Get oriented at the Frank Lloyd Wright–influenced **Beaver Meadows Visitor Center**. **Trail Ridge Road** is open from late May to mid-October; worthwhile stops include the 4-mile **Ute Trail** and the **Alpine Visitors Center**, the highest-elevation visitor center in the entire national park system. Visit in September or "Elk-tober" to see bugling elks during mating season.

Black Canyon of the Gunnison National Park

IN 1999, PRESIDENT Bill Clinton signed an act that made Black Canyon of the Gunnison into a National Park, and it still has a lot to celebrate as it heads into its third decade. In September 2015, it was named one of the first International Dark Sky Parks. That same year, a private philanthropist bought 79 acres and donated it to the park—two years later, another 2,494 acres of private land were added.

The starring act of the park is Black Canyon itself, notable for being a triple threat: deep, steep and narrow. The winning combination, carved out over 2 million years by both the Gunnison River and weathering, has created a spectacular gorge, located about 73 miles southeast of Grand Junction, Colorado.

The view from above can be seen from drives on both sides of the rim. The path to the North Rim Road starts with a gravel road and leads to six overlooks, while the 7-mile South Rim Road has 12 scenic points, including Gunnison Point, Chasm View, Painted Wall and Sunset View.

Hiking trails on both sides—which are 1,100 feet apart at the narrowest point at the rim level—cater to all levels and lengths, from the 0.6-mile easy Cedar Point Nature Trail, featuring views of the 2,250-foot high Painted Wall (the state's tallest cliff), to the 5-mile Deadhorse Trail, an old service road known for its birding.

For those hoping to experience the view from the Gunnison River, the road may be difficult, but possible. Drive down via **East Portal Road** into the **Curecanti National Recreation Area** which has campgrounds and fishing. Just beware of the 16-percent-grade steep road down the way. Hiking the inner canyon is also an option, even though the paths are unmarked. Multiple options are available from every direction, including the **S.O.B. Draw** from the North Rim, **Gunnison Route** from the South Rim and **Devil's Backbone Route** from the East Portal.

Black Canyon had been a national monument since 1933; a desire for conservation led to it being named a National Park.

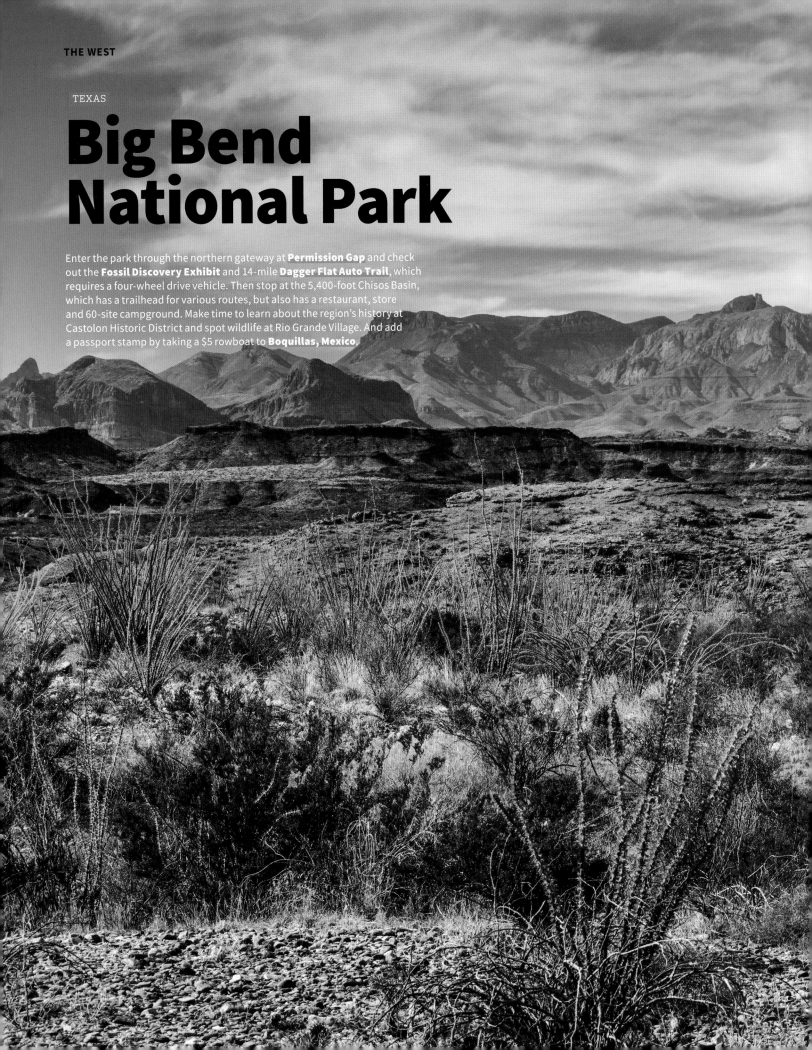

TEXAS

Big Bend National Park

Enter the park through the northern gateway at **Permission Gap** and check out the **Fossil Discovery Exhibit** and 14-mile **Dagger Flat Auto Trail**, which requires a four-wheel drive vehicle. Then stop at the 5,400-foot Chisos Basin, which has a trailhead for various routes, but also has a restaurant, store and 60-site campground. Make time to learn about the region's history at Castolon Historic District and spot wildlife at Rio Grande Village. And add a passport stamp by taking a $5 rowboat to **Boquillas, Mexico**.

LOCATED IN ONE of the most remote parts of the United States, the 800,000 acres of Big Bend National Park in the Chihuahuan Desert can be a challenge to get to. You'll have to drive 300 miles from El Paso, 412 miles from San Antonio or 540 miles from Dallas. Even the closest commercial airport, Midland/Odessa, is still about 200 miles away. Or you can take the Amtrak Sunset Limited, which runs three days a week and is about 80 miles north of the western entrance. No matter how you arrive, you'll see plenty of Texas—and the rewarding views are well worth the journey.

About 400,000 visitors do make it every year to Big Bend, which is the only National Park to encompass an entire mountain range, the Chisos, and be bordered to the south by the Rio Grande Wild and Scenic River. The isolation is part of the appeal, along with the sites that are 100 percent Texan, like the Castolon adobe structures, former candelilla-wax manufacturing site Glenn Spring and the abandoned Mariscal Mine.

Unwind at the Chisos Mountains Lodge, with 72 rooms right at the park's center, or go more rustic at a campground or RV park. Once you've found your home base, enjoy the middle-of-nowhere feel by hiking on the roadless public lands, backpacking through the backcountry, paddling down the Rio Grande or driving along the 100 miles of paved roads and 150 miles of unpaved ones. And for bird watchers, this is prime territory since its location on the 100th meridian places it right on the migration route.

A May 2019 fire burned 1,300 acres of the park and destroyed two historic adobe buildings near Castolon.

TEXAS

Guadalupe Mountains National Park

The park features 80 miles of hiking trails. Its signature trail, up to **Guadalupe Peak**, climbs 3,000 feet in 8.5 miles. Get a photo op by the monument at the peak and sign the logbook. The full **McKittrick Canyon Trail** rambles 5 to 7 miles round-trip, but less experienced hikers can get a taste on the easier 0.9-mile **McKittrick Canyon Nature Trail**. The best views of the **Capitan Reef** are found on the 4.2-mile **Devil's Hall Trail**. The park operates two information centers, as well as two campgrounds: one at **Pine Springs**, the other at **Dog Canyon**.

UNLIKE MANY NATIONAL parks whose peak visitor season occurs during the summer, Guadalupe Mountains National Park shines in the autumn, when its scenic McKittrick Canyon comes alive with fall colors. Together with limestone canyon walls and lazy McKittrick Creek, the scene is considered the most beautiful spot in all of Texas.

Beyond McKittrick Canyon, other wonders await—the four highest peaks in the state, as well as the well-preserved Capitan Reef, the largest Permian fossil reef in the world. Part of the Guadalupe Mountains, this 260-million-year-old ridge was once covered by sea. Highpointers (those aiming to climb the highest summits in each of the 50 U.S. states) make a beeline for 8,749-foot Guadalupe Peak, the "rooftop of Texas."

Regardless of the destination, visitors keep watch for the varied wildlife, from birds of prey such as golden eagles and peregrine falcons to nocturnal desert dwellers like coyotes, kit foxes, bobcats, mountain lions and badgers. Black bears, elk, gray foxes, skunks, mule deer and porcupines inhabit the park's higher elevations.

After dark, stargazers can easily observe more than 11,000 stars, as well as the Milky Way. The sight is a well-earned reward for those intrepid enough to camp out in this Wild West wilderness—and concrete proof that the stars at night are indeed big and bright, deep in the heart of Texas.

There are 60 species of mammals in Guadalupe.

Starry Parks

Five International Dark Sky Parks (IDSP) for admiring the heavens

Black Canyon of the Gunnison National Park

During the day, look 2,000-plus feet down into "Colorado's own Grand Canyon," which stands out for its combined narrowness, sheerness and depth. After dark, look up into the park's primordial dark sky, which received an IDSP designation in 2015, thanks in part to its summertime astronomy talks and festival.

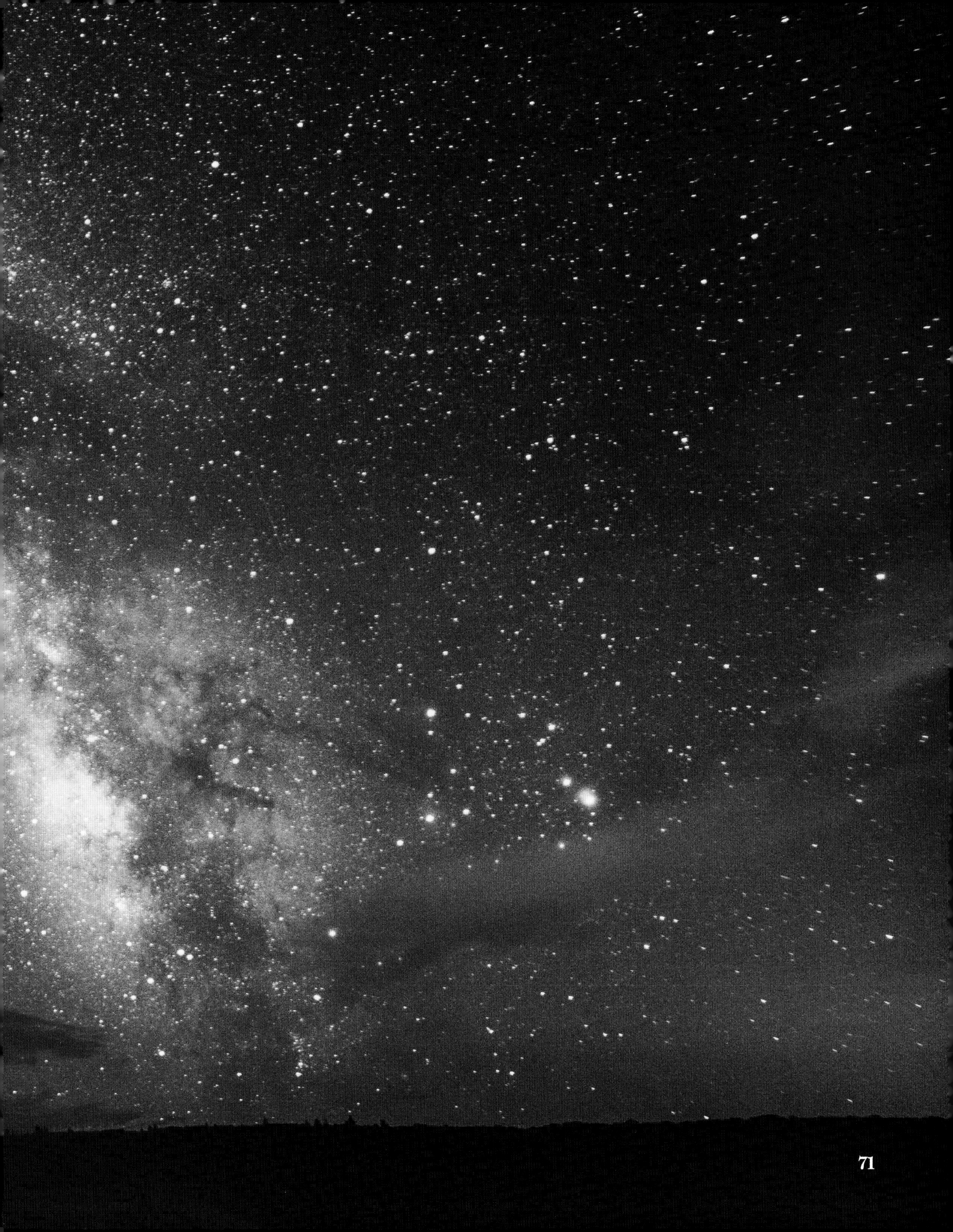

Capitol Reef National Park

In Capitol Reef's Cathedral Valley, sunrise and sunset illuminate Glass Mountain (left) and the sandstone monoliths known as the Temples of the Sun and Moon. In the evening, park staff—in partnership with the National Park Service Night Sky Team—shed light on the cosmos with night-sky tours, full-moon hikes, storytelling and more. The Heritage Starfest takes place every fall.

Great Basin National Park

Great Basin, in remote east-central Nevada, is a park of layers—subterranean caves, vast desert, high-elevation forest, rugged mountains and, above it all, a blanket of stars. Visitors can even join "dark rangers" aboard the Star Train, with a stop to view planets, meteors, star clusters, satellites, the Milky Way, the Andromeda Galaxy and other deep-space objects.

NEVADA

TEXAS

Big Bend National Park

Protecting the largest portion of the Chihuahuan Desert in the U.S. as well as some of the Rio Grande and the entire Chisos Mountain range, Big Bend can reach temps upward of 100 degrees in the summer. Things cool off at night, so you can gaze comfortably at coal-black skies, the Milky Way and 2,000 stars.

Canyonlands National Park

Famous for its Mesa Arch, Canyonlands is a labyrinth of stair-stepping canyons, dramatic mesas and weathered pinnacles, all sculpted by the Green and Colorado rivers. After dusk, ranger programs and telescope viewing shift visitors' attention to the lightscape above—a galaxy of stars and even the rings of Saturn.

3
CHAPTER

CALIFORNIA

With the most national parks of any state in the union (nine),
America's first preserved land (Yosemite) and an
incredible landscape of peaks, deserts, coasts and cliffs,
it's no wonder the Golden State attracts dreamers.

Soaring mountains
and roaring rivers
stretch out for
miles at Sequoia
National Park.

Sequoia National Park

SEQUOIA TAKES NATIONAL
Parks to new heights—literally. Mount Whitney, on the far eastern border, is the tallest mountain in the contiguous United States, while the General Sherman Tree is the world's largest tree at 275 feet tall, with a 36-foot diameter.

While the park is often linked with the adjacent Kings Canyon National Park, it's Sequoia that can boast about its Giant Forest grove, where General Sherman sits. On a plateau between the Kaweah River's Marble and Middle forks, the area has "more exceptionally large sequoias than any other grove," according to the National Park Service.

The 2-mile Congress Trail leads you through a tour of some of the most impressive specimens. The big-name trees here mean that crowds come to feel dwarfed by the natural giants, but for a quieter path, try the two-mile hike from Generals' Highway to Muir Grove, which has its own impressive concentration of full-grown sequoias.

For a winding journey from the foothills to the groves, take the hour-long drive from Generals' Highway from the entrance to Lodgepole, with stops to catch views of the California's Coast Range and the flat granite Beetle Rock along the way.

Hidden in plain site are also more than 200 caves, including the marble Crystal Cave, which can be seen on a guided visit (hint: buy tickets at least two days in advance). Tours range from a 50-minute family-friendly excursion to the half-day, off-trail Wild Cave Tour, which requires belly-crawling through narrow passages and over steep drop-offs.

One of the most symbolic icons of the park is giant domed **Moro Rock**, which can be reached via a 350-step stone staircase. Also worth a visit is the smaller dome **Little Baldy**, accessible from a 1.7-mile trail with some steep switchbacks. For a gentler pathway, head to **Big Baldy** and cruise along a ridge going up about 600 feet over its 2.2 miles.

When this sequoia fell in 1937, park workers realized it was easier to cut this hole through it than to chop it apart.

Kings Canyon National Park

IF THE CROWDS AT YOSEMITE turn you off, consider this neighbor to the south. Lying alongside Sequoia National Park in the southern part of the Sierra Nevada mountain range, the centerpiece of the park is the namesake canyon—which lives up to its royal name as the country's deepest canyon at a mile-and-a-half deep.

On the 45-minute drive starting at Grant Grove, you'll go from sequoia groves through numerous viewpoints, including Canyon View pullout, which offers a bird's-eye view of the U-shaped geography of the stunning canyon. Also worth a visit along the route are the marble-and-volcanic rock layered Boyden Cave, the cascading veils of Grizzly Falls, the powerful Roaring River Falls gushing through a narrow chute, and the 1.5-mile loop trail around Zumwalt Meadow.

At the bottom of the canyon is Cedar Grove, 35 miles east of Grant Grove. While the area is less frequented, the sites are just as mesmerizing, most notably the 8,717-foot North Dome and 8,518-foot Grand Sentinel, as well as the mighty Kings River.

Originally called General Grant National Park (after the 267-foot-tall General Grant tree dubbed the "Nation's Christmas tree"), President Franklin D. Roosevelt designated Kings Canyon as a National Park in 1940. It has been operated along with Sequoia National Park since World War II. While Sequoia gets to brag about having the tallest tree, Kings Canyon has the largest sequoia grove on the planet, Redwood Canyon.

Enter the park from the Big Stump entrance on Highway 180 and head 3 miles east to Grant Grove to find the **Kings Canyon Visitor Center**. Divided into two distinct sections—Grant Grove and Cedar Grove—the former offers lodging at the **John Muir Lodge** or timber-style **Grant Grove Cabins**, while the latter offers nourishment at the **Cedar Grove Market and Snack Bar**.

Swimming and fishing— and in some cases, boating— are among the activities available in Kings Canyon.

CALIFORNIA & NEVADA

Death Valley National Park

Forays into Death Valley begin at the **Furnace Creek Visitor Center**. Four resorts—**Stovepipe Wells Village**, **Panamint Springs Resort**, **The Ranch at Death Valley** and the historic **Inn at Death Valley**—as well as eight NPS campgrounds operate within the park. Combine a visit with stops at nearby national parks **Kings Canyon** and **Sequoia**. Travel to Death Valley during the summer is not advised.

Death Valley reached 134 degrees in July 1913—the highest temperature ever recorded on Earth.

EXTREME HEAT, EXTREME dryness, extreme depth—it's all here in Death Valley, the largest U.S. national park outside of Alaska and the hottest, driest place in North America.

Established as a national monument in 1933 and redesignated a National Park in 1994, Death Valley dips as low as 282 feet below sea level at Badwater Basin, the lowest point in North America. The protected salt flats here are among the largest in the world, covering almost 200 square miles. Sometimes filled with surreal puddles and pools, they're all that's left of a prehistoric lake.

On the way to Badwater, worthwhile side trips beckon: the much-photographed Zabriskie Point, overlooking the arid, ridged badlands; Golden Canyon's arcing Red Cathedral rock formation; Devil's Golf Course, an expanse of rock salt eroded into spiky stacks; and the striped sedimentary hills of Artist's Palette.

Elsewhere, visitors can climb 100-foot mounds of sand in Mesquite Flat Dunes and walk the rim of 600-foot Ubehebe Crater. The more intrepid can venture to Wildrose Canyon to see 10 hive-shaped charcoal kilns dating to the 19th century.

Christened in 1849 by gold prospectors struggling through the region, Death Valley is surprisingly full of life, supporting hundreds of plant and animal species. The remarkable adaptations developed to survive such an extreme environment are yet another example of the park's many marvels.

Redwood National and State Parks

Many visitors head in from US 101, also known as the aptly named **Redwood Highway**, which runs north from the **Golden Gate Bridge** and winds its way through the length of the park. Stop in at the **Kuchel Visitor Center** to get a look at the history of the park or take part in a ranger-led nature walk. At the town of **Orick** on the banks of **Redwood Creek**, find guided kayak trips, horseback rides and mountain biking options—as well as the popular summer **Orick Rodeo**.

ALONG WITH THE Statue of Liberty and the Grand Canyon, the soaring trees that form cathedral-like groves in this national park are among America's most iconic symbols. Actually comprised of a national and three state parks, the 130,000-acre preserve is home to one of nature's greatest wonders: The Sequoia sempervirens, the tallest living tree on Earth, can reach a height of 379 feet and a diameter of more than 29 feet. (Redwoods are also among the oldest living things on Earth, dating back thousands of years.) While the trees are the stars, black bears, coyotes, bobcats, cougars, elk, deer, river otter and sea lions also vie for your attention here.

In addition to over 200 miles of hiking trails, you can horseback ride or mountain bike in certain areas and kayak or canoe along the 40-mile seacoast or Smith River. Fisherman may want to try their luck at hooking a salmon or steelhead trout. Sadly, over 96 percent of the old-growth redwoods have been logged; though a massive replanting project is underway, it will take 250 years for the saplings to grow to even a modest size. Still, as John Steinbeck wrote in *Travels With Charley: In Search of America*, "Once seen, [redwoods] leave a mark or create a vision that stays with you always."

SOUTHERN CALIFORNIA

Channel Islands National Park

ONE PARK, FIVE ISLANDS, 145 indigenous plant and animal species: This is why Channel Islands National Park has earned the moniker "the Galápagos of North America." An adventurous spirit and advance planning are prerequisites to visiting this 390-square-mile evolutionary outpost off the coast of Southern California, but the effort is well worth it, especially for wildlife enthusiasts.

Designated in 1980, the park is only reachable by plane or boat. Santa Cruz and Anacapa are the most accessible isles, with ferry service running year-round (two hours round-trip).

The most traversed, Santa Cruz Island is fit for day trips or family-friendly camping. Water lovers can snorkel kelp forests and kayak through sea caves near Scorpion Beach. Sightseers should also hike to Cavern Point for a panorama of the coast, keeping an eye out for wildlife like scrub jays and island gray foxes.

Anacapa is lined with sea caves, natural bridges and rugged cliffs—from the ferry, travelers must climb 157 stairs to reach the crest of the island. Cathedral Cove and Pinniped Point are the places to spy sea lions and harbor seals lounging on the shore.

While the islands' isolation may be the reason the park sees fewer than 350,000 annual visitors, it's also what allows adventurers to walk in Darwin's footsteps, discovering flora and fauna found nowhere else on Earth.

No entrance fee is required, but you will have to pay for a boat or plane charter. **Island Packers** ferries depart from **Oxnard** and **Ventura**, where the park's main visitor center is located. **Channel Islands Aviation** offers flights from **Camarillo**. Go during whale-watching months: late December through April for gray whales; June through September for humpbacks and blue whales. There are no cars, restaurants, shops or lodging on the islands. The park's more remote islands may require a permit or be closed due to current conditions.

A hike to Inspiration Point on Anacapa Island affords a view of 40-foot Arch Rock.

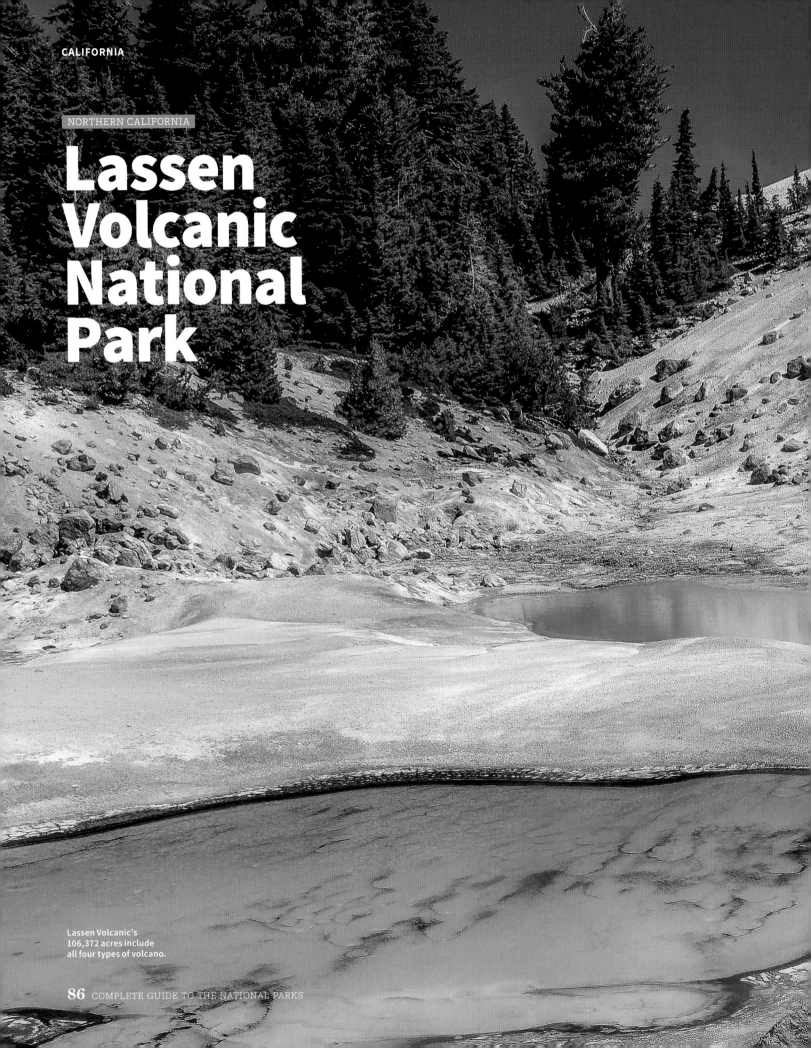

NORTHERN CALIFORNIA

Lassen Volcanic National Park

Lassen Volcanic's
106,372 acres include
all four types of volcano.

AROUND THE EDGES of the Pacific Ocean lies the Ring of Fire—a series of seismic sites and volcanoes, including legends like Mount Fuji and Mount Saint Helens. A lesser-known member of the ring is Lassen Peak, which last erupted in 1914 and remains one of the largest plug dome volcanoes in the world.

Now dormant, the peak headlines Lassen Volcanic National Park, created in 1916. Intrepid souls can trek 5 miles up to the 10,457-foot summit, but more casual admirers get the signature view from the shores of Manzanita Lake.

Lassen Peak shares the spotlight with a plethora of bubbling mud pots, rumbling steam vents and boiling springs. The best place to observe this noisy (and smelly) phenomena is Bumpass Hell, named after Kendall Bumpass, the pioneer who discovered the area in the 1860s—and purportedly lost a leg after falling into a hot spring. Visitors take in this bizarre 16-acre landscape on a 3-mile boardwalk stroll.

Contrasting the volcanic terrain is the Shasta Cascade's cooler side— alpine lakes, breezy meadows and crisp waterfalls. From coniferous forests to smoking fumaroles, Lassen Peak towers over it all. The imposing volcano is a powerful reminder that in this volatile land, you don't play with fire.

The park offers one lodge—60-room **Drakesbad Guest Ranch** (open early June through mid-October)—and eight campgrounds, including the most popular one at **Manzanita Lake**, the hub of the park. Don't miss the 1.5-mile scenic loop trail around the shore. The closest alternative accommodations are in **Plumas County**. Start your adventure at the **Kohm Yah-mah-nee Visitor Center**, close to the southwest entrance.

SOUTHERN CALIFORNIA

Joshua Tree National Park

Reach new heights by rock climbing: The park has 8,000 climbing routes and 2,000 boulder challenges for adventurers of all levels. **Joshua Tree Guides** offers daily four-hour rock climbing technique classes ($250 for one, $200 each for two, $150 each for three or more) and two-day big-wall climbing courses ($595 for one, $495 each for two). For beginners, **Joshua Tree Rock Climbing School** has one-day classes for $195.

MINERVA HAMILTON HOYT was born on a Mississippi plantation and raised as a Southern belle. Even after she got married and moved to Southern California, she stayed in high-society circles—and developed a love for the native desert plants in the area. Thanks to her conservation efforts, 825,000 acres were set aside and proclaimed as Joshua Tree National Monument in 1936 by President Franklin Delano Roosevelt—and eventually gained full National Park status by the California Desert Protection Act in 1994 (which also expanded the park another 234,000 acres).

The Park's namesake tree is a desert treasure: a succulent type of yucca tree and a member of the agave family, covered in spiny leaves that come to a sharp point. It is said that Mormon travelers in the mid-1800s gave the trees their common name after the biblical figure of Joshua—their branches reminded them of Joshua's arms raised in prayer. The tallest Joshua tree in the park is more than 40 feet tall and can be found in the Queen Valley Forest.

Joshua Tree National Park has over 200 miles of roads, 191 miles of hiking trails, 523 campsites, nine solar-power stations—and even two horse camps. Sitting about 140 miles from Los Angeles, it's become an easy weekend escape—and Instagram hot spot—with about 1.2 million people visiting each year.

Two desert systems—Mojave and Colorado—meet inside the park.

Pinnacles National Park

Pinnacles was signed into law as a National Park in 2013.

HIGH ABOVE THE SALINAS Valley soar North America's largest flying birds, California condors, with wingspans of up to 9.5 feet. The sight is near-miraculous, as condors have been endangered since 1967 and the population dwindled to just 22 birds in the 1980s. Thanks to captive-breeding programs, California condors are making a comeback, and today, Pinnacles National Park co-manages 86 of these wild scavengers.

A national monument since 1908, Pinnacles also protects an unusual geologic formation that dates back 23 million years. An ancient volcano created the park's domes, crags and spires; then, over the ages, earthquakes and other tectonic forces carried these breccia-rock formations 195 miles along the San Andreas Fault to their present resting place.

Some 32 miles of hiking trails zigzag through the 26,000-acre park. Visitors flock to the Bear Gulch Cave Trail (1.5 miles), which passes through two talus caves (rocky tunnels). The 1-mile Moses Spring Trail is another favorite.

For the best views, hikers scramble up the High Peaks Loop (6 miles round-trip), which winds through narrow passageways and a labyrinth of boulders to an elevation of 2,720 feet. Below, Pinnacles' rugged expanse of rolling plains and hulking monoliths unfolds. Above stretches an endless sky— and, with luck, a graceful condor, riding the thermals far above its rare and fascinating habitat.

The park has two entrances (east and west), which aren't linked by roads. The only campground is located at the east entrance. Find additional lodging and restaurants in the town of **Salinas**. Rock climbing is popular here; companies like **Adventure Out** offer clinics for all experience levels. Travel between March and May to see the park's wildflower display—and to avoid summer's 100-plus-degree temps.

NORTHERN CALIFORNIA

Yosemite National Park

JOHN MUIR ONCE SAID, "Keep close to nature's heart...and once in a while climb a mountain or spend a week in the woods. Wash your spirit clean." The "father of our national parks" may have been calling to mind one of his favorites, Yosemite.

Four million people descend on this UNESCO World Heritage site each year to see Yosemite Falls, North America's tallest waterfall; El Capitan, the world's tallest granite monolith; and the towering sequoia trees, the oldest living things on Earth.

The Ahwahneechee Indians called Yosemite home for 4,000 years before a group of pioneers arrived in 1833. Soon after, stories of the heart-stopping vistas swelled as quickly as the cascading waterfalls. Rapid development got the attention of conservationists, who petitioned Congress to protect the area. In 1864, President Abraham Lincoln signed the Yosemite Grant, making Yosemite the first land set aside for preservation by the U.S. government and laying the groundwork for future National Parks—it officially became one in 1890.

Quintessential Yosemite sites include Half Dome, whose sheer cliff is the largest in North America, moonbows (lunar rainbows) that put on a kaleidoscopic nighttime light show, and the Mist Trail, which climbs 1,900 feet.

Yosemite welcomes all who wish to wash their spirits clean, as Muir urged, and a week here won't seem long enough.

While Yosemite sprawls over 1,169 square miles, visitors traverse only a fraction.

Tunnel View is Yosemite's most iconic vista.

Yosemite National Park is open 24/7/365, but avoid holiday weekends. Plan your visit in early spring, right as the snow is starting to melt, for some of the best waterfall action. When it comes to getting around, take advantage of the free shuttles that run throughout the park, as well as the 12 miles of bike trails in the valley. Built in 1927, the **Ahwahnee hotel** (restored to its original name after some years as The Majestic Yosemite Hotel) endures as the premier lodge in the Yosemite area.

Breathtaking Trees

From ancient pines to towering redwoods, here's where to hug a tree in California

Joshua Tree National Park

Every year, more than 2.5 million people make the pilgrimage to see Joshua Tree's namesake flora, *yucca brevifolia*. Growing up to 40 feet tall, the park's Joshua trees thrive at between 2,000 feet and 6,000 feet and sprout white-green flowers in the spring. Get the money shot at Black Rock Canyon, Indian Cove or Queen Valley Roads.

Mariposa Grove, Yosemite

More than 500 mammoth trees stretch toward the sky in the Mariposa Grove of Giant Sequoias, located in Yosemite's southernmost region. A variety of trails takes you past such stunners as the 3,000-year-old Grizzly Giant, the massive Fallen Monarch and the California Tunnel Tree (below)—which has a pathway carved into the base so you can walk right through it.

Muir Woods National Monument

Just 12 miles north of the Golden Gate Bridge and administered as part of the Golden Gate National Recreation Area lies what naturalist John Muir called "the best tree-lover's monument that could possibly be found in all the forests of the world." Six miles of walking paths weave through the last grove of old-growth coast redwoods in the Bay Area.

Ancient Bristlecone Pine Forest

At more than 4,000 years old, Inyo National Forest's ancient bristlecone pines are the oldest trees on the planet. Walk the boardwalks and trails surrounding the visitor center at Schulman Grove, then make your way to Patriarch Grove, home to the Patriarch Tree, the world's largest bristlecone pine.

Giant Sequoia National Monument

Just outside the borders of Sequoia National Park, this national monument—established by President Bill Clinton in 2000—protects 33 groves of giant sequoias, which often grow more than 20 feet wide. Don't miss the Boole Tree, the only giant sequoia spared from logging in Converse Basin and one of the largest trees on Earth.

Badlands National Park lies mostly between the Cheyenne and White rivers in South Dakota.

CHAPTER 4
THE MIDWEST

Though perhaps not as epic as the great parks out West, America's heartland flaunts its own kind of beauty, from barren badlands and idyllic islands to mystic caves and verdant valleys.

SOUTH DAKOTA

Badlands National Park

Popular hikes in the park include the **Notch Trail** (1.5 miles round-trip) and the Castle Trail (10 miles). Get info at the **Ben Reifel Visitor Center**, close to the **Cedar Pass Campground** (primitive camping is available at the **Sage Creek Campground**). The historic **Cedar Pass Lodge** provides the only hotel lodging within park borders. Find alternative accommodations in **Rapid City**, an hour's drive away. If you have more time, head over to the park's **Stronghold** and **Palmer Creek** units, part of the Pine Ridge Indian Reservation of the Oglala Sioux.

The remarkably striped
badlands were once an
ancient seabed.

Shale, sand, gravel,
iron oxides and volcanic
ash tinted the badlands'
colorful sediment.

WHEN THE LAKOTA PEOPLE first encountered Southwestern South Dakota's harsh terrain, they called it *mako sica*—"land bad." Today, however, the intensely eroded pinnacles, buttes, fins and spires of Badlands National Park are some of its greatest assets.

Created in 1978, the park welcomes nearly 1 million annual visitors who come to behold its pyramid-like rock formations. The backbone of the park's topography is the Wall, a 60-mile escarpment that tells a story of erosion millions of years in the making. Day-trippers can savor views of the Wall and other vistas along the 30-mile Badlands Loop State Scenic Byway, while short hikes on the Door and Window trails get adventurers up close.

Other marvels range from the largest mixed-grass prairie in the U.S. to prolific wildlife. Bison, pronghorn, deer, prairie dogs, coyotes, snakes, eagles and hawks are often seen from Sage Creek Rim Road.

Perhaps even more impressive is the park's paleontology—Badlands National Park holds the planet's richest fossil beds from the Oligocene epoch. Aspiring archaeologists can get their bearings on the Fossil Exhibit Trail, then freely explore the park searching for prehistoric relics (all fossils must remain in the place they were found). Surely, after happening across the ancient jaws of a three-toed horse or saber-toothed cat, there will never be any question that these badlands are indeed full of goodness.

SOUTH DAKOTA

Wind Cave National Park

Bison were reintroduced to the area in 1913 and are now thriving.

IN THE BLACK HILLS OF South Dakota lies a park with a split personality. One side is sunny, open, full of life. The other: dark, mysterious and deeply spiritual. The latter whistles to passersby, enticing them to step inside and see the wonders within.

This twofold place is Wind Cave National Park, where the world's sixth-longest cave hides beneath ponderosa pine forests and mixed-grass prairie lands teeming with wild animals.

Most visitors come to explore the park's namesake cave, whose whistling sound (produced by changes in atmospheric pressure) led to its modern discovery by two brothers in 1881. It became America's eighth national park in 1903, but it has long been revered as sacred by the Lakota people.

Rangers host five different tours inside the cavern, ranging from 30 minutes to four hours in length. Notably, the Fairgrounds Tour (which lasts 1.5 hours) reveals the cave's outstanding boxwork formations, the best and most extensive example of these thin calcite honeycombs on the planet.

An entirely different world waits above ground. Sixty percent of the park's 28,295 acres is open prairie, and wildlife-spotters regularly spy bison, elk, pronghorn and prairie dogs from park roads.

Outside the car, 30 miles of trails include the hike to 5,013-foot Rankin Ridge, the highest point in the park. Here, visitors savor sweeping vistas of the Black Hills, while knowing Wind Cave's shadowy secrets lie just under the surface.

Wind Cave is a one-hour drive from **Rapid City**. Tickets for ranger-led cave tours must be purchased from the visitor center. Arrive early and dress warmly (the cave is 54 degrees year-round). The **Elk Mountain Campground** is the park's only campground. Lodging and other amenities are available in the surrounding towns of **Hot Springs** and **Custer**.

NORTH DAKOTA

Theodore Roosevelt National Park

The park operates two campgrounds within its borders—**Cottonwood** in the South Unit (near **Medora**) and **Juniper** in the North Unit (near **Watford City**). Additional lodging is available in each nearby town. Both units have a year-round visitor center, and the South Unit runs a second center during the summer. Popular activities include horseback riding and paddling down the **Little Missouri River**. Contact park rangers before traveling to the **Elkhorn Ranch** site.

Rugged badlands and wild horses are classic sights in this stark park.

WHILE PRESIDENT, TEDDY Roosevelt set aside more than 200 million acres of land for preservation—arguably the most any president has done for the National Park Service. And it was his time in North Dakota that sparked his passion for conservation. He first traveled to the territory that is now Theodore Roosevelt National Park to hunt and ranch cattle, and the area proved to be a salve after he lost both his wife and his mother on the same day in 1884.

Today visitors can still see Roosevelt's Maltese Cross Cabin and wander the site of his Elkhorn Ranch. Designated a national park in 1978, TRNP memorializes the 26th president while protecting 70,000 acres of prairie grasses, rolling buttes and painted badlands, all along the Little Missouri River.

Most visits begin in the park's South Unit, where the 36-mile Scenic Loop Drive winds past 12 trailheads and pull-offs like the popular Painted Canyon Overlook. This section also boasts a petrified forest and prolific wildlife, including prairie dogs, bison, deer, pronghorn, badgers and elk.

The North Unit, 70 miles away, has its own 14-mile scenic byway, with stops such as the River Bend and Oxbow overlooks. Between the two units, the 218-acre Elkhorn Ranch site sees the fewest visitors. Here, Roosevelt himself might be pleased to learn this remote riverside plot remains as pristine as it was the day he first saw it.

Hot Springs National Park

Drinking the hot-springs water is safe and encouraged, so visitors should "quaff the elixir," as they used to say in the spa's heyday—and bottle some to take home. Fountains are located near the corner of **Central Avenue** and **Reserve Street**, and in **Hill Wheatley Plaza**.

FITTINGLY CALLED THE
American Spa, Hot Springs is the birthplace of the modern quest for wellness. Much of this unique national park sits within Hot Springs' city limits, where people have tapped into the mineral-rich waters since Egyptians were building the pyramids.

Rainwater from more than 4,000 years ago still flows through the springs, surging back up from the Earth's crust so rapidly that it doesn't have time to cool. Native Americans originally settled near what they called the Valley of the Vapors, and Spanish explorer Hernando de Soto rediscovered the springs in 1541, sending word back to Europe that a fountain of youth had been found in the New World. The area became an official national park in 1921.

Today, 1 million visitors come to bathe in the same waters as former presidents, prohibition-era mobsters, major-league baseball players and the elite jet set of yesteryear. At Buckstaff Bathhouse on Bathhouse Row, spa-goers slip into the thermal waters, which heat naturally to 143 degrees, before entering a steam room.

Other musts in Hot Springs include a trip to Hot Water Cascade, where the rocks are thick with rare blue-green algae; a drive along Hot Springs Mountain Drive; and a hike across Sugarloaf Mountain on the Sunset Trail.

In a world of overpriced facials and massages, a return to the earth at the American Spa might be just what the doctor ordered.

A mere 5,550 acres, Hot Springs is the country's smallest national park.

MINNESOTA

Voyageurs National Park

More than one-third of Voyageurs' area is water.

Minnesota's sole National Park, Voyageurs is the only inland water-based park in the entire National Park System.

VISITORS TRADE WHEELS for hulls in Voyageurs National Park—a 218,054-acre swath of the U.S.–Canada border. Canoes, kayaks, motorboats and houseboats ply the park's four large lakes (Rainy, Kabetogama, Namakan and Sand Point) and 26 smaller lakes, linked by narrow channels.

All told, the park holds fewer than 10 miles of roads and more than 80,000 acres of lakes and waterways. Thirteen designated visitor-destination sites illuminate the area's colorful past, from the French-Canadian fur traders who paddled birch-bark canoes through the region in the late 18th and early 19th centuries (*voyageurs* means "travelers" in French) to the bygone resort era of the 1930s.

Modern-day voyageurs hungry for nature can behold Rainy Lake's 80-foot granite cliffs at Anderson Bay (one of the most-photographed spots in the park) or Sand Point Lake's 125-foot bluff at Grassy Bay (one of the highest points in the park). Hikers can ramble on 27 miles of trails (the Cruiser Lake Trail, which crosses the Kabetogama Peninsula, is a favorite for moose-spotting). And casual observers can wander through the historic Ellsworth Rock Gardens, where rock sculptures and terraced flower beds form a striking work of art.

Curiously, some of the oldest exposed bedrock on Earth is found within this relatively young national park, established in 1975. Sanded, shaped and scarred by at least four ice ages, the prehistoric land here tells a fascinating story. Those who pay close attention will hear it, along with the rustling of North Woods pines, the haunting cry of loons, the howling of wolves and, of course, the gentle lapping of pure, pristine water.

Find lodging, supplies, guide services and boat rentals in Voyageurs' gateway communities of **Orr/Pelican Lake**; **Ash River Trail/Kettle Falls**; **Crane Lake; International Falls**, **Rainier and Rainy Lake** and **Kabetogama Lake**. The park offers three visitor centers, as well as ranger-led canoe programs and sightseeing cruises. There is only one lodging option within the park—the circa-1913 **Kettle Falls Hotel**. Some 200 tent and houseboat sites are reachable only by boat. In the winter, go wild on 110 miles of groomed snowmobiling trails.

MICHIGAN

Isle Royale National Park

Isle Royale's lowest elevation is 601 feet, at Lake Superior.

IN THE MIDDLE OF the largest freshwater lake (by area) in the world lies an island so remote and rugged that it has no roads or cars, and travelers must arrive by boat or floatplane. This "eye" of Lake Superior is Isle Royale, a national park since 1940. The least-visited national park in the contiguous U.S., Isle Royale sees an average of only 18,000 people a year—and they must *really* want to come, as the ferry ride from park headquarters in Houghton, Michigan, takes six hours.

Once there, passengers are rewarded with solitude, serenity and pristine North Woods scenery. Visitors to the more populous Rock Harbor area can board the *Sandy* to cruise past sights like the circa 1855 Rock Harbor Lighthouse. On foot, hikers head for picturesque Scoville Point via the Stoll Trail (4.3-mile loop), named after journalist Albert Stoll, who fought to preserve the island.

Sightseers bound for the Windigo area can paddle or dive into the invigorating waters of Washington Harbor. Throughout the park, trekkers explore 165 miles of trails, keeping their eyes peeled for 20 elusive mammal species, including moose, beaver, red fox, mink, river otters, snowshoe hares and gray wolves.

While visits to most national parks average only four hours, those who make the long journey to Isle Royale (open April 16–October 31) typically stay four days. It's a testament to the permeating allure of the park's isolation and unspoiled natural beauty.

Ferry options include the NPS-operated *Ranger III* from **Houghton**, Michigan (six hours); the *Isle Royale Queen IV* from **Copper Harbor**, Michigan (3.5 hours); and **Grand Portage Isle Royale Transportation Lines** in **Grand Portage**, Minnesota (1.5 hours). Alternately, arrive courtesy of **Isle Royale Seaplanes**. On-island lodging includes 36 primitive campgrounds, the **Rock Harbor Lodge** and the **Windigo Camper Cabins**.

OHIO

Cuyahoga Valley National Park

During the winter months, **Boston Mills** and **Brandywine** ski resorts operate within the park, and the **Towpath Trail** remains unplowed for cross-country skiing. From late April through October, the **Countryside Farmers Market at Howe Meadow** peddles fresh foods, arts, crafts, flowers and more every Saturday. To stay within the park, there are two options: the nine-room **Stanford House** and the six-room **Inn at Brandywine Falls**.

CUYAHOGA VALLEY NATIONAL Park is one of the most-visited national parks in the country—so why haven't many people heard of it? Chances are, if you don't know about this park, tucked in Ohio's northeastern corner between the cities of Cleveland and Akron, it's because you don't live in the Buckeye State: Only 20 percent of park users hail from outside state borders. For those in the know, the park's varied attractions are pure delight.

The centerpiece of Cuyahoga Valley is the Ohio & Erie Canal Towpath Trail, which cuts through the park for 20 miles (the full trail is 85 miles). Stops along the way include visitor centers, 11 trail heads and the Beaver Marsh boardwalk.

Nature lovers flock to the Ritchie Ledges (towering sandstone cliffs) and 65-foot Brandywine Falls. Quirkier diversions range from the Blossom Music Center and the Porthouse Theatre, to several golf courses and the Cuyahoga Valley Scenic Railroad.

The Cuyahoga River Valley was named a National Recreation Area in 1974. To further define the landscape, it became a National Park in 2000. A brand-new visitor center opened in 2019, giving curious travelers even more reason to check out this scenic local celebrity.

Indiana Dunes National Park

Enter the park from Exit 31 off the Indiana Toll Road and stop at the **Indiana Dunes Visitor Center**. Tucked in the park are 60 historic homes, including the **Bailly Homestead**; this National Historic Landmark is the 19th-century home of Honore Gratien Joseph Bailly de Messein, who helped develop this region of Indiana and set up the only trading post between Chicago and Detroit. Also in the area are the **Chellberg Farm**, which belonged to a Swedish immigrant family at the turn of the 19th century, and the three-story **House of Tomorrow**, which assumed every family would own an airplane.

THE NEWEST ADDITION to the National Park system is Indiana Dunes, which officially earned its status on February 15, 2019, after a century-long attempt.

Formerly known as Indiana Dunes National Lakeshore, the 15,000-acre park sits along 15 miles of Lake Michigan's southern shore with forest, dunes, marshes and prairies along with 50 miles of hiking paths. Since joining the National Park ranks, tourism has risen in the area to the highest levels in eight years.

The vast shoreline makes the lakefront beaches a popular destination, which has been named a top-five family beach getaway by *Parents* magazine. Each of the eight beach areas offers a different experience. At Lake Front or Kemil Beach, enjoy a walk by historic homes from the 1933 Century of Progress World's Fair along Lake Front Drive, while Portage Lakefront and Riverwalk Beach has a 1.5-mile paved waterfront trail along the Burns Waterway, leading to views of the Great Lake.

The best known of the dunes for which the park is named is Mount Baldy, which sits 126 feet above the lake level. However, the dune itself is currently considered "starving" since beach erosion is removing more sand than is coming in. To combat its demise, the Army Corps of Engineers has been "feeding" the dune since 1974. Still, winds more than 7 miles an hour cause the dune to shift, and Mount Baldy actually moves about 4 feet a year.

MISSOURI

Gateway Arch National Park

During your visit, also make time to browse the **Gateway Arch Museum**, which opened in 2018—and offers free admission. The exhibits cover the westward expansion of the United States and the role St. Louis played in it from 1764 to 1965, including sections on **Colonial St. Louis**, **Jefferson's Vision**, **Manifest Destiny**, **the Riverfront Era**, **New Frontiers** and the building of the **Gateway Arch**.

The structure
is exactly as wide as it is
tall—that is, 630 feet.

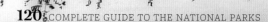

THE GATEWAY ARCH STANDS as a soaring symbol of Thomas Jefferson's vision to stretch the United States toward the west—and into the land that it is today. Towering 630 feet above the grassy fields of Gateway Arch National Park in downtown St. Louis, not only is it the world's tallest arch, but it's also the tallest memorial in the U.S. It's twice as tall as the Statue of Liberty and dwarfs the Washington Monument by 75 feet.

As for its innovative design? That's the work of Finnish-American architect Eero Saarinen, who won the hotly contested Jefferson National Expansion Memorial Competition in 1948. The seamless curve—made of 886 tons of stainless steel—was heralded as a way to honor the rich heritage of the city's past paired with a nod to the future. It took nearly two decades for Saarinen's original design to come to fruition—and, sadly, he never saw the finished product. In 1961, Saarinen died of a brain tumor at the age of 51, four years before workers installed the final exterior piece of the arch's facade.

Nowadays, a tram still takes visitors to the top of the arch, where views can expand for 30 miles.

Seeking to elevate the Arch experience, the $380 million CityArchRiver project—completed in 2018—ushered in changes including 11 new acres of park featuring 5 miles of bike and walking paths, and an outdoor natural amphitheater.

Lovely Lakes

The Midwest's lakeshores beckon
with bluffs, dunes and water activities galore

Pictured Rocks National Lakeshore

Named for its mineral-stained sandstone bluffs, this 42-mile stretch of Michigan's Lake Superior shoreline—from Munising to Paradise—was established as America's first national lakeshore in 1966. Beaches, waterfalls, historic lighthouses and eye-catching cliffs tempt travelers. Cruise past famous formations like 200-foot Grand Portal, the highest point on the shore.

MICHIGAN

Sleeping Bear Dunes National Lakeshore

Sandy beaches, inland lakes, coastal villages, serene rivers and, of course, towering dunes comprise this pretty area, designated a national lakeshore in 1970. Explore the park on foot, scaling up the popular Dune Climb, or by car on Pierce Stocking Scenic Drive (7.5-mile loop). The Lake Michigan Overlook lends 450-foot views of the world's fourth-largest freshwater lake.

MINNESOTA

Boundary Waters Canoe Area Wilderness

Located deep in northeast Minnesota and accessible primarily by canoe, this remote and beautiful wilderness extends 150 miles along the U.S.-Canada border, with more than 1,100 lakes and 1,500 miles of canoe routes. You'll need a permit to enter the area (find it at recreation.gov) but it's worth the red tape for a chance to get away from it all and explore.

Apostle Islands National Lakeshore

Made up of 21 islands and 12 miles of mainland shoreline, this archipelago holds more lighthouses (nine) than any other site in the NPS. In summer, visitors can cruise or paddle Lake Superior's clear waters. In winter, Apostle Islands' sea caves and cliffs transform into a frosted wonderland.

Cadillac Mountain is one of seven peaks that soar over 1,000 feet in Maine's Acadia National Park.

5

THE EAST

Water—seashores and watersheds, floodplains
and falls—defines many of the East Coast's
most spectacular sights, alongside pretty ranges like
the Great Smokies and the Blue Ridge Mountains.

127

MAINE

Acadia National Park

Visitors can hike to the summit of **Cadillac Mountain** (7.7-mile loop) or simply drive. Start your adventure at the **Hulls Cove Visitors Center**, and coast along the 27-mile **Park Loop Road**. Acadia has two campgrounds and no lodging, and many park roads close during the winter. Don't miss popovers and tea at the **Jordan Pond House** restaurant, open seasonally. More dining and lodging options are available in **Bar Harbor**. The hop-on/hop-off **Island Explorer** shuttle is free.

More than 3.3 million visitors a year come to admire Acadia's 40-plus miles of rocky shoreline.

FROM OCTOBER 6 to March 7 every year, the rising sun kisses Cadillac Mountain before any other spot in the U.S. At 1,530 feet, the famous summit is the highest mountain on the North Atlantic seaboard—and its home is Acadia, the first national park to open east of the Mississippi.

Elsewhere on Mount Desert Island, visitors can walk the Ocean Path from Sand Beach to Thunder Hole, where waves entering a partly submerged sea cave boom like thunder at certain times of day. Farther on, Otter Cliff's 110-foot granite bluff grants epic ocean views.

Some 24 pristine ponds, including serene Jordan Pond, dot the glacier-carved interior. And weaving through the park's 48,000 acres are 45 miles of car-free carriage roads, funded by John D. Rockefeller Jr. from 1913 to 1940.

Rockefeller and affluent summer residents donated land that would become Sieur de Monts National Monument in 1916. Redesignated Lafayette National Park in 1919, it took its current title in 1929. Today, Acadia is a household name, and the landscape is considered the crown jewel of the North Atlantic Coast.

Built of brick in 1858, Bass Harbor lighthouse is the only one on Mount Desert Island.

VIRGINIA

Shenandoah National Park

LOCATED 75 MILES WEST OF Washington, D.C., Shenandoah National Park is less about the destination and more about the journey—one that starts on its main thoroughfare, Skyline Drive. The National Scenic Byway winds 105 miles along the crest of the Blue Ridge Mountains, with 75 lookout points along the way. To the east are the foothills of Virginia's Piedmont region; to the west, the Shenandoah Valley. But who constructed this snaking road that more than 1.4 million visitors drive each year?

After the Depression, the Civilian Conservation Corps was formed as part of the New Deal program. Men from the Corps worked in the park to build the highway, along with scenic overlooks, campgrounds, trails and several structures now listed on the National Register of Historic Places. They also planted the foliage lining the road—Fraser firs, red spruces, table-mountain pines—that bursts into fiery colors come fall.

To truly experience the glory of the park's nearly 200,000 acres, visitors should set off on foot. More than 500 miles of hiking trails range from simple to strenuous—and include 105 miles of the famed Appalachian Trail. Walks lead up mountains, down canyons and past streams, historic landmarks and old homes that once belonged to the area's settlers, who were relocated before Shenandoah was designated as a national park in 1935. The most popular—and risky—hike is Old Rag Mountain (9 miles round-trip), involving a rock scramble to its 3,284-foot summit and lofty view.

Several trails lead to waterfalls, including 93-foot Overall Run Falls, the tallest cascade in the park (6.4 miles round-trip). Alas, the hike's climb of 1,850 feet happens on the way back. But once in the car, driving one of the most scenic routes in the U.S., it's easy to forget the trek uphill.

Leaf-peeping season (around mid-October) is the park's busiest time.

Four park entrances are located along **Skyline Drive**, as well as two visitor centers, at mile 4.6 and mile 51. Lodging options include guest rooms, suites and cabins at **Lewis Mountain** (mile 57.5), **Skyland** (mile 41.7) and **Big Meadows** (mile 51). While it's smart to enter the park with a full tank, mile 51 does have a gas station. Restaurants and grab-and-go food options are available at Skyland and Big Meadows.

Shenandoah sits along the Blue Ridge Mountains, one of the oldest and most accessible ranges in the world.

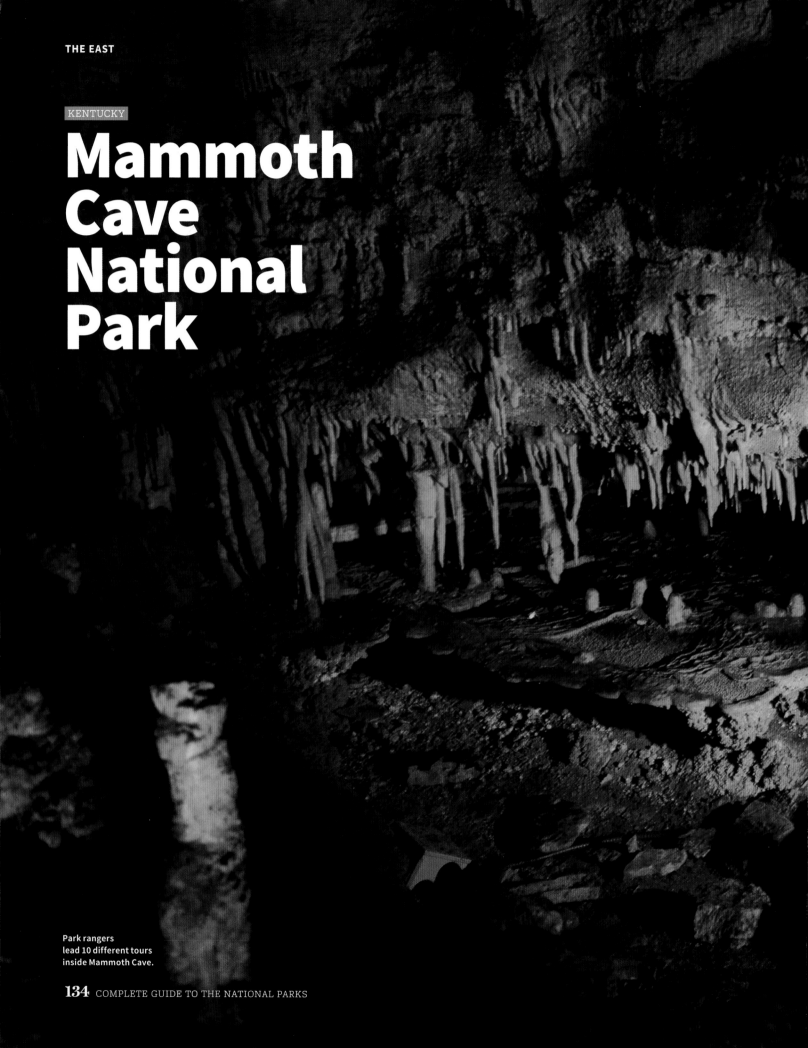

KENTUCKY

Mammoth Cave National Park

Park rangers
lead 10 different tours
inside Mammoth Cave.

TUCKED INSIDE THE EARTH within the Green River Valley lies Mammoth Cave, where more than 400 miles of mapped cave—and innumerable unexplored passageways—make it the longest cavernous system in the world.

The first souls entered Mammoth Cave 4,000 years ago and used it for shelter and gathering minerals. European hunter John Houchins is credited with rediscovering the cave around 1800. Settlers used it as a source of saltpeter for gunpowder during the War of 1812, as well as a tuberculosis hospital in the 1840s. Throughout the 19th and early 20th centuries, slaves mapped the majority of what has been explored in Mammoth Cave and acted as guides for early tourists.

Lanterns light the way as modern cavers pass pleated drapes of limestone and a staggering dripstone formation called Frozen Niagara. Around each craggy corner, other sights emerge: the Snowball Room, where large white balls of gypsum cover the ceiling, and Devil's Looking Glass, a slab of stone on which early explorers drew charcoal petroglyphs.

More discovery awaits aboveground: 70 miles of hiking and biking trails, as well as water-play on the Green River.

Mammoth Cave became a National Park in 1941 and was later declared a UNESCO World Heritage site and an International Biosphere Reserve. This labyrinthine karst draws more than 600,000 annual visitors eager to uncover its secrets.

It's about 54 degrees inside the cave, and plenty of spots hold water, so wear a sweater and shoes that can get wet. Choose from several cave tours that vary in difficulty; some include upward of 500 stairs. Three developed campgrounds and the **Lodge at Mammoth Cave** operate inside the park.

Great Smoky Mountains National Park

WHAT MAKES GREAT Smoky Mountains National Park the country's most visited, welcoming more than twice the number of people as any other park in the system? Is it the park's location, less than a day's drive from nearly everywhere in the East? Its free admission? Its status as a UNESCO World Heritage site, an International Biosphere Reserve and the largest area of protected land east of the Rockies?

Arguably, the park's distinctive beauty is the greatest attraction. Ridge after ridge fades into the horizon, exuding a smoky haze—the product of organic compounds let off by the area's dense flora.

Three main entrances are jumping-off points for forays into the national park, established in 1934. From Gatlinburg, Tennessee, the Sugarlands Visitor Center equips travelers to explore scenic landmarks like Laurel Falls, Rainbow Falls and the Alum Cave Bluffs.

Farther west, the town of Townsend, Tennessee, is the gateway to the popular Cades Cove valley. Here, an 11-mile loop road takes sightseers past abundant wildlife, as well as the historic cabins, churches and mills of early Southern Appalachian settlers.

And from North Carolina, U.S. Route 441 connects the town of Cherokee to the Oconaluftee Visitor Center, where a sprawling collection of historic buildings depicts everyday life on a 19th-century farmstead.

In the heart of the park, the 6,643-foot Clingmans Dome observation tower is the highest point in Tennessee. The vista—reaching from the vast Smokies into seven states beyond—brilliantly captures the area's glory. From this transcendent viewpoint, it's easy to see why GSMNP is America's favorite.

Can't choose among the 800 miles of trails? Try **Andrews Bald** (3.6 miles round-trip), **Charlies Bunion** (8 miles round-trip) or 100-foot-high **Ramsey Cascades**, the park's tallest waterfall (8 miles round-trip). Some 71 miles of the **Appalachian Trail** also cut through the park. The **Cataloochee Valley** is the place to see elk, which were successfully reintroduced to the area in 2001. Inside the park, stay at **LeConte Lodge**, accessible only by hiking. Or camp at one of 10 developed campgrounds. Twelve neighboring communities, including charming **Bryson City**, offer additional amenities.

The Great Smokies boast 90 historic structures, 100 waterfalls and 100,000 types of flora and fauna.

Visitors frequently spot black bears, coyotes, wild turkeys, groundhogs, deer and raccoons in Cades Cove, the most-visited area of the park.

SOUTH CAROLINA

Congaree National Park

The biggest bald cypress in the park (and state) measures 127 feet tall.

TREES ARE THE SUPERSTARS of this unlikely national park in central South Carolina, home to the largest old-growth hardwood forest in the Southeast. With an average canopy height of over 100 feet, the park contains 25 trees that are the largest of their respective species in the state—including a 167-foot-tall loblolly pine that's also the biggest tree of its kind in the country.

These arboreal giants were attractive to loggers in the 1890s, but because of the area's inaccessibility, the work was halted. A group of conservationists worked to officially protect the site, which became a national monument in 1976. National Park status came in 2003, and some 143,000 annual visitors explore this floodplain forest.

Sightseers can hike several flat trails that start at the visitor center. The Boardwalk Loop Trail (2.4 miles) weaves between massive water tupelo trees, oaks and maples. Deer and wild turkeys can be spotted on the Oakridge Trail (6.6 miles), while the Weston Lake Loop Trail (4.4 miles) leads to Cedar Creek, home to otters and wading birds.

Throughout the park, explorers can spot knobby cypress knees. Legend holds that these woody growths are elves that spring to life after dark—though even inanimate, they're a fascinating sight in this wet woodland.

Congaree is a 30-minute drive from downtown **Columbia**, where you can find lodging and gear rentals. BYO canoe, or reserve a ranger-guided tour of the **Cedar Creek Canoe Trail**. Visit May through October for the best hiking conditions, as the trails are usually flooded during other months of the year. Bug spray is a must: The park has a mosquito meter ranging from 1 (All Clear) to 6 (War Zone). Spring and fall offer the best weather and fewer pests.

139

WEST VIRGINIA

New River Gorge National Park & Preserve

While there's only primitive camping in the park, many of the surrounding towns offer lodging. Nearby **Hawks Nest** and **Pipestem Resort State Parks** also have lodges, while **Babcock** and **Bluestone State Parks** offer cabin rentals. For more, go to **newrivergorgecvb.com**.

The third Saturday of October is Bridge Day at New River; activities include BASE jumping, rappelling and concerts (with food vendors).

IT'S OUR NEWEST national park (it was designated one in December 2020, part of a pandemic relief bill), but paradoxically, it's also one of the oldest places in the country: The river that twists and turns so dramatically through the park's center is thought to be the second oldest on Earth; fossil evidence suggests it could be 320 million years old.

Fast-forward a few epochs, and today the New River, which drops 750 feet over 66 miles, draws whitewater rafters who brave the Lower New, a 13-mile stretch of Class IV and V rapids. Meanwhile, the steep canyon walls beckon rock climbers, who rate the 1,500 climbing routes as among the best on the East Coast.

Prefer your vacations with less of an adrenaline rush? Hike trails that range from ¼ to 7 miles, or ride a bike on the 12.8 miles of Boy Scout–built paths. You can also kayak, canoe or take a (commercial) boat trip on the more placid stretches of the river.

Also not to be missed: a drive to Sandstone Falls, a 1,500-feet-wide waterfall with a maximum drop of 36 feet; the route takes you past scenic outlooks, trailheads and historic sites that are reminders of when the 73,000-acre park was home to hundreds of mining hamlets, many of which are now ghost towns. Also noteworthy: the African American Heritage Auto Tour route, which highlights the role Black families played in making this area the center of coal production. The park also lies in the north-south flyway for migratory birds; be on the lookout for bald eagles and peregrine falcons.

FLORIDA

Everglades National Park

Florida's dry season (December through April) is the time to go, with better weather, more wildlife, fewer mosquitoes and more ranger programs and park amenities available. Four visitor centers are worth a stop. Pitch a tent at **Long Pine Key** or **Flamingo** campground. Find hotels and adrenaline-fueled airboat tours in **Homestead** and **Everglades City**.

AMERICA'S THIRD-LARGEST national park has no mountains, no glaciers, no geysers. A vast, shallow watershed, it flows quietly, imperceptibly, for 100 miles, emptying into Florida Bay. Tucked in its endless marshes are 400 kinds of birds, more than 20 threatened wildlife species and the most extensive mangrove ecosystem in the Western Hemisphere. This 1.5 million–acre area is Everglades National Park, the largest designated subtropical wilderness reserve in North America.

Human development threatened to destroy the Everglades in the early 1900s, but advocates came to the rescue, and Everglades National Park was born in 1947.

Three unconnected entrances grant access. In Shark Valley, 35 miles from Miami, a park tram travels the 15-mile loop road, and a 65-foot observation tower lends 360-degree panoramas of the saw grass prairie and its wildlife.

Along the Gulf Coast south of Naples, Everglades City is the launch pad for narrated boat tours of the pristine Ten Thousand Islands. Here, too, experienced paddlers embark on the 99-mile-long Wilderness Waterway Trail.

To the south, the town of Homestead is the gateway to the remote Royal Palm and Flamingo areas. In Royal Palm, day-trippers walk the Anhinga Trail, where alligators and tropical birds are spotted by the dozens. Boardwalk trails and guided canoe trips lead explorers deeper into the Everglades in and around Flamingo, the southernmost spot in mainland Florida.

While animal lovers won't find the grizzlies and other large mammals of the West here, they may be lucky enough to spot the endangered manatee, American crocodile or Florida panther. In this famous "river of grass," it's a different type of discovery, but an unforgettable adventure all the same.

FLORIDA

Biscayne National Park

You'll definitely need a boat to get beyond the **Dante Fascell Visitor Center**, but guided tours—from sightseeing to snorkeling to diving—depart from there daily. There is no park entry fee, unless you take a guided excursion or dock overnight to camp on **Boca Chita** or **Elliott**. **Adams** is day-use only. Visit between December and May to avoid hurricane season.

AT BISCAYNE NATIONAL PARK, the main trail is for snorkeling, not hiking. Sturdy boots are traded for swim fins, and boats, not cars, are the main method of transportation.

The 173,000-acre preserve stretches from Key Biscayne to Key Largo, and 95 percent lies peacefully underwater. But this park— which sees 508,000 annual visitors and shelters the world's third-largest coral barrier reef—was almost destroyed in the 1950s.

Developers envisioned hotels and highways and proposed dredging 8,000 acres and a 40-foot-deep channel through the bay. Conservationists lobbied to protect the site, including Herbert W. Hoover Jr., who took congressmen on blimp rides to showcase the bay's beauty. The creation of Biscayne National Monument in 1968 halted any further

construction, and national parkhood was achieved in 1980.

Explorers boat-hop to the uninhabited keys dotting the landscape, as well as the three main islands: Adams, Elliott and Boca Chita, the most popular. Also worth an excursion: the seven overwater shacks of Stiltsville, which has a storied Prohibition-era past.

The main attraction is the Maritime Heritage Trail, which accesses prime snorkeling and diving spots, such as the circa-1878 Fowey Rocks Lighthouse. Buoys also mark six shipwrecks, including the Erl King. In the winter, lucky paddlers spy manatees in the turquoise waters—a prize for journeying to this watery wonderland.

Boca Chita's 65-foot ornamental lighthouse looks across to Miami.

FLORIDA

Dry Tortugas National Park

SURPRISE! KEY WEST is not the most western island in Florida. Quietly sitting another 70 miles west is the remote Dry Tortugas National Park. The seven-island park isn't just known for its natural wonders by land and by sea—it also contains one of the country's largest forts, dating back to the 19th century. Located on the park's second-largest island (the 14-acre Garden Key) is Fort Jefferson, which was built to watch over the Gulf of Mexico and the Straits of Florida.

Seemingly in the middle of nowhere, the location actually sits along one of the busiest shipping lanes in the world. While the army abandoned it in 1874, it was later used as a coaling station for warships. And it had its moment in the spotlight in 1898, when the *USS Maine* left from the fort for Havana and was sunk, leading to the Spanish-American War.

The largest island, Loggerhead Island, is named for the loggerhead turtles that frequent the area. Snorkeling here also reveals numerous shipwrecks, including the Windjammer Wreck, a steel-hulled sailing vessel that sank in the early 1900s. Another impressive snorkel site is the coral reef at Little Africa Reef— named after its shape, which resembles the continent.

Accessible only by ferry or seaplane, the only way to stay overnight in the Dry Tortugas is by camping at the Garden Key campground, south of Fort Jefferson. But planning ahead is key, as it's first-come first-served—and only 10 campers a day are allowed on the *Yankee Freedom III* ferry to get there.

To reach the **Dry Tortugas**, check the ferry schedule from Key West for the *Yankee Freedom III* (note the annual maintenance in late October and early November, when the boat doesn't run) or seaplane by **West Seaplane Adventures**. With no fuel, water or food service in the park, careful planning and packing is required. Also check out the smaller islands like **Bush Key**, home to bird species not found anywhere else in the country.

The Windjammer Wreck is the final resting place of the *Avanti*, which struck a reef and sank in 1907.

147

Luminous Lighthouses

These guiding lights have become icons in their own right

Portland Head Light

CAPE ELIZABETH

Plans for what is now one of the country's most photographed lighthouses started in 1787 with just $750, but eventually received more funding when it was commissioned by George Washington and dedicated by Marquis de Lafayette. The original 72-foot-tall structure first shined its light in 1791. Sitting on rocky cliffs in the 90-acre Fort Williams Park, the conical tower is accompanied by a Victorian-style keeper's home.

MASSACHUSETTS

Great Point Light

NANTUCKET

Located inside the Coskata-Coatue Wildlife Refuge are 16 miles of trails that wind through a diverse landscape, including salt marshes, sand dunes and coastal forests, as one well as one of the highlights—the Great Point Light. The white concrete lighthouse stretches 70 feet into the sky at the intersection of Nantucket Sound and the Atlantic Ocean. The trip there on soft sand is well worth the challenge, since it's located about 10 miles round trip from paved roads.

Tybee Island Light Station

TYBEE ISLAND

Georgia's tallest and oldest lighthouse rises 145 feet, surrounded by three Light Keeper's Cottages. Commissioned by James Oglethorpe in 1732, the general called it "the best building of that kind in America." Admission to the 3-acre site includes a climb up 178 steps to the top of the black-and-white tower (don't worry, there are resting platforms with a viewing window every 25 steps), as well as a visit to a raised cottage and the Tybee Museum.

Cape Hatteras Lighthouse

BUXTON

Right off the shore of Cape Hatteras is one of the most treacherous parts of the Atlantic Coast, where the Gulf Stream runs into the Virginia Drift. But here, the 90-foot sandstone Cape Hatteras Lighthouse bravely stands. The original height and signal of the 1803 structure wasn't strong enough, so by 1870, a new 150-foot-structure was built in its place. Now the black-and-white striped tower is 208 feet tall—the tallest in the country, according to the American Society of Civil Engineers.

NORTH CAROLINA

Block Island North Light

BLOCK ISLAND

The shifting sands of Block Island have always made construction in the Sandy Point area a challenge. But the result of the fourth attempt was the Block Island North Light, dating back to 1867, at the end of Corn Neck Road.

The path to the lighthouse starts by Settler's Rock—inscribed with the names of families who settled in the area in the 1600s—and leads through a half-mile walk to the granite building.

RHODE ISLAND

Visitors often head to Hawaii's Haleakala National Park crater at dawn and sunset to enjoy the view.

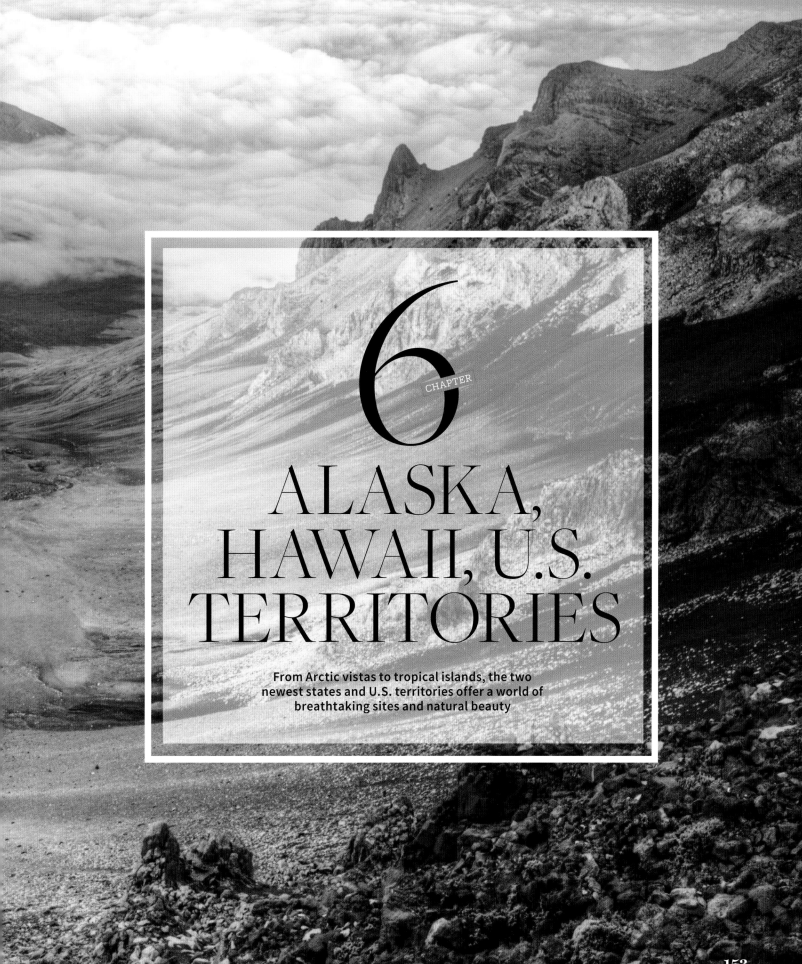

6

CHAPTER

ALASKA, HAWAII, U.S. TERRITORIES

From Arctic vistas to tropical islands, the two newest states and U.S. territories offer a world of breathtaking sites and natural beauty

ALASKA

Denali National Park & Preserve

ONE OF ALASKA'S most-visited National Parks, this 6 million-acre wild landscape is dominated by the Alaska Range and the 20,310-foot-tall Denali, North America's highest peak. Climbers arrive regularly to tackle the mountain, while others enjoy the view of "the great one" from land. Only about 30 percent of visitors get lucky, because the peak is so often shrouded in clouds.

With only one restricted-access road in and out, most visitors take a bus deep into the park to explore its beauty and spot wildlife, namely Alaska's big five: bears, moose, caribou, Dall sheep and wolves. There are a handful of trails and campgrounds, but the vast majority of the park is undeveloped and experienced outdoors enthusiasts can roam a trail-less landscape.

In the summer, rangers lead daily hikes of varying difficulties and the park's kennels are also open for sled-dog demonstrations to learn how these canine rangers help survey the park. At the Murie Science and Learning Center, 70 million-year-old dinosaur fossils await—the first evidence of the giant reptiles in interior Alaska was discovered in the park in 2005.

Part of the magic lies in sitting back and taking in the awe-inspiring views and the immense history of this place: a homeland to the Athabascan people, a safe preserve for once-threatened wildlife—and a vast wilderness.

Glaciers cover a sixth of the park—that's 1 million acres. The longest is the 44-mile-long Kahiltna glacier.

While many travelers stay at hotels near the entrance of the park, there are a few lodges inside the park for those who want to immerse themselves in the wilderness. The family-owned **Sheldon Chalet** is the newest and most luxurious, with electricity, running water and fine dining. The hexagon-shaped lodge, with just five guest rooms, sits 10 miles from the summit of **Denali** at 6,000 feet. Go snowshoeing, glacier trekking or wait for the northern lights.

Kenai Fjords National Park

The **Kenai Fjords National Park Visitor Center** is located in Seward, the main portal to the park. During the summer, the **Alaska Railroad** connects **Seward** and **Anchorage**. May to September is the optimal time to go, with calmer seas, longer days and road access to **Exit Glacier**. Don't miss a half- or full-day outing to the fjords and coastal islands; boat tours launch from Seward daily.

IMAGINE AN ICE FIELD so immense it covers 700 square miles, so dense it's up to a mile thick, so powerful it feeds almost 40 glaciers, and so ancient it dates back 23,000 years. This is Kenai Fjords National Park's Harding Icefield, one of only four ice fields left in the United States—and the largest one located completely within U.S. borders.

While Harding Icefield is the most impressive feature of the park, Exit Glacier is the most accessible. This half-mile-wide band of ice is in the only section of the park that's reachable by road from the town of Seward —and a half-hour hike brings visitors up close.

Along the park's southern reaches, the Gulf of Alaska draws boatloads of gawkers to its frosty fjords, where thousands of seabirds nest, neon-blue icebergs drift and eagle-eyed visitors spy sea otters, harbor seals, Steller's sea lions, orcas, Dall's porpoises and humpback whales.

Those even hungrier for adventure can kayak amid the subarctic scenery. Aialik Bay is a popular destination for paddlers, who earn box seats to the symphony of pops, booms and shudders that result as the ice face cracks and calves nearby.

Other activities range from fishing, biking and beachcombing to skiing, snowmobiling and dogsledding—area pastimes that predate the park's official establishment in 1980 as part of the Alaska National Interest Lands Conservation Act.

Visitors can also keep their eyes peeled for 27 species of land animal. Mountain goats scale steep cliffs, moose wade through waterways, and black bears slide down snow chutes. It seems the Kenai Peninsula is every bit the playground for wildlife as it is for humankind.

Ice and snow blanket 60 percent of Alaska's smallest national park (607,000 acres).

Bear Glacier Lagoon is paradise for kayakers and stand-up paddleboarders.

ALASKA

Lake Clark National Park & Preserve

Port Alsworth, the main gateway to the park, offers guides, gear rentals, a visitor center and lodging, such as **Farm Lodge**. Several air-taxi services make the one-hour flight to Port Alsworth from **Anchorage**. Though the park is open year-round, summer is the best time to visit, when temps hover in the 50s and 60s.

BLUE GLACIERS. STEAMING volcanoes. Wild rivers. Turquoise lakes. Hulking bears. Lake Clark National Park takes the best Alaska has to offer and condenses it all into 5,625 square miles.

Created in 1980, Lake Clark sweeps from the coast of Cook Inlet, over the spine of the Chigmit Mountains, to the alpine tundra of the interior. Yet despite its diverse beauty, the preserve receives only 21,000 visitors a year. Most enter through Port Alsworth, a small community on the east shore of Lake Clark. Here, trailheads lead to the Tanalian trails network—the only maintained trail system in the park— with day hikes to Tanalian Falls and the peak of 3,570-foot Tanalian Mountain.

The highlight of Lake Clark is its namesake lake. Fifty miles long, brilliantly aqua and surrounded by snow-capped mountains, it's a popular spot for canoeing, kayaking and fishing. Elsewhere in the park, outfitters facilitate float trips on the preserve's three Wild and Scenic rivers. The water presents unique opportunities to view Lake Clark's 37 species of land mammals, including the Mulchatna herd of more than 100,000 caribou. Along the coast, travelers spot beluga whales, harbor seals, sea otters and puffins (inset, right).

Even within its more-trafficked areas, the park remains one of the least visited in the entire NPS—ensuring a pure, peaceful and exclusive encounter with Mother Nature.

Lily pads carpet the park's Silver Salmon Lake.

Kobuk Valley National Park

THIRTY-FIVE MILES ABOVE the Arctic Circle lie the largest arctic sand dunes in the world. Formed 14,000 years ago as retreating glaciers ground rocks into sand, the Great Kobuk Sand Dunes, together with two smaller dune fields, cover 30 square miles. The place to see this geologic curiosity is Kobuk Valley National Park.

Established in 1980, the 1.7 million-acre park gets its name from the Kobuk River valley that cuts through its center. Sixty miles of this wide waterway (Kobuk means "big river" in Inupiaq Eskimo) run within park borders. Flanking the valley are the Baird and Waring mountains, as well as boreal forest and treeless tundra.

No trails exist in the park, except those blazed by migrating Western Arctic caribou, the largest herd of the species on Earth. However, visitors (only 15,500 in 2016) rarely spot the park's elusive wildlife. Most merely fly in for the day to picnic on the peculiar dunes. Still, even this brief encounter is one for the books, as travelers set foot on a wild landscape unchanged for millennia.

Some dunes in
Kobuk Valley National Park
rise as high as 100 feet.

Learn about Kobuk Valley at the **Northwest Arctic Heritage Center** in **Kotzebue**, the closest major town with air service to and from Anchorage. From Kotzebue, air-taxis touch down on the dunes or the **Kobuk River**; there are no roads or facilities inside the park. As Kobuk Valley is only 32 miles west of **Gates of the Arctic National Park**, some tour operators offer combined river/hiking trips with time in both locations.

Remnants of the Pleistocene era, Kobuk Valley's bizarre sand dunes mirror those found on Mars.

Gates of the Arctic National Park & Preserve

From February to April, the northern lights flicker over Gates of the Arctic's rugged Brooks Range.

NO ROADS, NO TRAILS, no facilities, no other souls— Gates of the Arctic National Park is one of the last untamed places on Earth.

Established in 1980, the northernmost national park in the United States sits entirely above the Arctic Circle and spans the Brooks Range, America's most northerly mountain chain and the terminus of the Rockies. Conservationist Robert Marshall christened the area the "Gates of the Arctic" in 1929, when he first glimpsed Mount Boreal and Frigid Crags mountain bounding the North Fork of the Koyukuk River. Today, the Gates are one of the few named landmarks in this epic 8.5 million-acre wilderness, along with six National Wild and Scenic rivers: North Fork Koyukuk, Alatna, John, Kobuk, Noatak and Tinayguk.

Private float trips ply these waters, and beyond their shores, guided backpacking tours take trekkers deep into the backcountry, immersing the truly adventurous in the scenic Arrigetch Peaks ("fingers of the hand extended," in native Eskimo). Seasonal wonders also grace this region: 30 days of endless sun in the summer; 490,000 caribou— Alaska's largest herd—migrating across the autumn-hued tundra; the northern lights dancing across the winter skies.

Photographers have a field day with the unspoiled natural beauty; the luckiest capture some of the preserve's four-legged residents (brown and black bears, wolves, Dall sheep, moose, musk ox, wolverines, arctic foxes) on film.

The photos—and the memories they represent—become precious keepsakes from a bold and extraordinary venture into the wild.

The least-visited national park in the entire system, Gates of the Arctic sees only 10,000 visitors a year.

From **Fairbanks**, several small carriers fly into the gateway community of **Be**... where the national park operates a visitor center. Lodges such as **Bettles Lodge**... accommodations as well as complete trip packages. Booking with a lodge or ou... is a must; **Alaska Alpine Adventures** leads both rafting and backpacking itiner... **Iniakuk Lake Wilderness Lodge** offers two rustic cabins within park bound...

Katmai National Park & Preserve

IN 1912, THE largest volcanic eruption of the 20th century rocked a far-flung corner of southern Alaska. Nearly 2 feet of ash descended on Kodiak, 100 miles away, but not a soul was lost. Explorer Robert Grigg returned to the site four years later. Seeing thousands of vents steaming from the valley floor, he christened it the "Valley of 10,000 Smokes"— and championed the 1918 campaign to protect Katmai as a national monument.

Today, Novarupta Volcano is dormant, and the Valley of 10,000 Smokes is forever preserved within the borders of Katmai National Park, established in 1980.

The volcano isn't the only draw within the park—over time, the region's brown bears have moved into the spotlight. Numbering over 2,000, they make up the world's largest population of the species—and spectators at Brooks Falls can witness up to 60 bears at a time feasting on the annual deluge of salmon just 30 yards away.

Most of the park's 37,000 annual visitors come for this spectacle, but an entire world of discovery, from lowland tundra to immense lakes, awaits in this remote playground. It's a poignant reminder that in this untamed patch of the world, Mother Nature rules.

Brown bears are North America's largest land predators—males can weigh upward of 1,000 pounds.

The heart of the park, **Brooks Camp** is accessible via floatplane from **Anchorage**, **Dillingham**, **Homer**, **King Salmon** and **Kodiak**. The NPS staffs a visitor center, ranger station and ranger-led programs here from June 1 to September 18. All arriving visitors must attend a bear-safety presentation. There is limited camping at Brooks Camp; concessionaire **Katmailand** also operates three lodges. Pack for wind, rain and chilly temps.

Wrangell-St. Elias National Park & Preserve

Get info and plan backcountry forays at the **Kennecott Visitor Center**, set in a historic red schoolhouse. Cabins, B&Bs, campsites and small lodges are available in and around **McCarthy-Kennecott**, as are outfitters for fishing, river rafting, mountaineering, glacier trekking and aerial tours.

Created in 1980, Wrangell-St. Elias National Park is covered with snow year-round.

WRANGELL-ST. ELIAS IS A LAND of superlatives. America's largest national park. The biggest designated wilderness area in the U.S. Home to the nation's largest glacial system, North America's most expansive subpolar ice field and the tallest coastal mountains on Earth.

What does all this mean for its visitors, who number just 80,000 a year? That this remarkable 13 million-acre treasure is still waiting to be discovered.

Travelers arrive via one of two primitive roads: Nebesna or McCarthy. The first stop is McCarthy-Kennecott, a historic mining town that boomed briefly when two prospectors discovered copper in the area in 1900. Walking tours explore the ghost town and abandoned mine, and several trails lend easy access to two of the park's 150-plus glaciers, Kennicott and Root.

To truly gain perspective on the vastness of the preserve—which could fit almost six Yellowstones within its borders—a flight-seeing tour is essential. Passengers stare open-mouthed at the convergence of four mighty mountain ranges: the Wrangells, the St. Elias, the Alaska and the Chugach. Vistas of countless glaciers, braided rivers and spongy tundra also stretch endlessly.

Wrangell-St. Elias' ranges hold nine of the 16 highest peaks in the United States—no wonder the park is nicknamed the "mountain kingdom of North America." Curious adventurers would do well to visit this immense high country now, while it's still a hidden gem.

169

ALASKA

Glacier Bay National Park

ENCOMPASSING 3.3 MILLION acres of Alaska's Inside Passage, Glacier Bay is more than a National Park. It's a living laboratory of the workings of Mother Nature. As a globally protected Biosphere Reserve (a site to study sustainable development), "it is a land reborn, a world returning to life, a living lesson in resilience," as the park's site describes.

Case in point: After naturalist John Muir visited the park in the late 19th century and noticed that glacial ice found by 18th-century visitors had retreated, Dr. William Skinner Cooper was inspired to study the development of plants in the newly exposed land, known as plant succession, in 1916. Now, a century later, scientists are still continuing the research, finding willows, alder and spruce in the region.

After all, 250 years ago, the entire park was covered by a single tidewater glacier. Retreat started around 1750 and has now moved back 60 miles. The natural process has created 1,045 individual glaciers, most of which start at an elevation between 8,000 and 15,000 feet. The largest of these is the 35-mile long Grand Pacfic Glacier, which has been steadily receding. Thankfully, others like the 21-mile long Margerie Glacier and 12.5-mile long Johns Hopkins Glacier are stable. The evolving glaciers mean pieces often break off in the form of icebergs—which harbor seals use as a safe place to give birth.

The only road into the park is from the town of Gustavus, 10 miles away—and that's only accessible via a 30-minute flight from Juneau, so most visitors enter from cruise ships and tour boats.

Since the bulk of the park is water, one of the best ways to experience Glacier Bay is by boat, whether by kayak, private charter or cruise ship. On land, head to **Bartlett Cove**, where a 100-mile-long glacier stood 200 years ago. It's the only developed area in the park, offering walks along the **Forest Trail**, visits to the **Xunaa Shuká Hít** (roughly translated as Huna Ancestors' House, which reflects the traditional architectural style of the Huna Tlingit home) and stays at the **Glacier Bay Lodge**.

Glacier Bay averages about 100 feet of snow annually, making it one of the world's snowiest places.

HAWAII

Haleakalā National Park

In the Summit District, enjoy the 0.4-mile **Pā Kaʻoao Trail** to see ancient rock-wall shelters and views of the crater, or opt for the full-day 11-mile **Keonehe'ehe'e Trail**, which crosses the crater. In the Kīpahulu District, head out on the 0.5-mile **Kūloa Point Trail** from the Kīpahulu Visitor Center to catch a Hawaiian cultural demonstration, and then soak in the coastal views at Kūloa Point.

LEGEND HAS IT that the demigod Maui wanted days to last longer so much that he stood on top of the volcano Haleakalā, threw a lasso and captured the sun so it would remain in the sky.

The tall tale does have one element of truth: Everything at Haleakalā revolves around the utmost respect for the sun. In fact, the name itself means "house of the sun" in Hawaiian— and every morning, the top of the peak is packed with visitors who gather to witness the sunrise in all its glory. The sunrise views are so popular that reservations are now needed 60 days in advance in order to preserve the area during its most popular period, from 3 a.m. to 7 a.m. (While sunsets can be just as spectacular, reservations are not required at this time.)

The park is split into two main districts. The Summit District immerses you in the cradle of the volcano's peaks, wandering through cinder deserts and shrublands. Along the way, treat your nose to the delightful smells of 'āhinahina, or silversword, blossoms, which are so sweet they're said to resemble honey.

Meanwhile, the Kīpahulu District is the complete opposite experience. Located on the Hāna Highway 12 miles past the main town, the coastal views allow your senses to take in a wonderment like no other, especially when you set your eyes on views like the 400-foot high Waimoku Falls.

This dormant volcano sits at over 10,000 feet above sea level.

Hawaii Volcanoes National Park

Kīlauea's May 2018 eruption occurred several hours after a magnitude 5 earthquake hit the Big Island of Hawaii.

THE KĪLAUEA VOLCANO had been quietly continually erupting since 1983, but in May 2018, the Pu'u 'O'o crater collapsed, causing Kīlauea's most disruptive eruption in recorded history: So much lava flowed, it could have filled 320,000 Olympic-size pools. The devastation destroyed 700 homes and wreaked havoc on the Puna District of the Big Island.

One of the two active volcanoes within the Hawaii Volcanoes National Park, Kīlauea caused damage in the park that included rock falls, cracked roads, water line damage and wrecked buildings. While recovery efforts are still in progress, after a 134-day closure the bulk of the park is back to being open for visitors.

The 15th site to officially be named a National Park, in 1916, the 335,259-acre park was also designated an International Biosphere Reserve in 1980 and a UNESCO World Heritage Site in 1987. There's good reason for those honors: Stretching from sea level to a 13,677-foot peak, Hawaii Volcanoes includes seven diverse ecological zones, from coastal to alpine, and is home to 60 species that are endangered or threatened, like the hawksbill turtle and Hawaiian goose.

The Kīlauea and Mauna Loa volcanoes at the heart of the park provide much of the unique geology, like fumaroles, calderas, thermal areas and black-sand beaches. The Crater Rim Drive (page 176) and Chain of Crater Road explore the highlights.

For a deeper dive, visit the 116,000-acre Kahuku ranch—once one of the biggest cattle ranches in the state—or go backcountry hiking within its 130,000 acres of wilderness.

To best see the park, take the **Crater Rim Drive** by starting at the **Kīlauea Visitor Center**. Next, head less than a mile down the road to the **Steam Vents**, **Steaming Bluffs** and **Ha'akulamanu (Sulphur Banks)**. Proceed to take in the views from the **Kīlauea Iki Overlook**, 400 feet above the 3,000-foot wide crater, and the **Pu'u Pua'i Overlook**, named after the gushing hill. Then go for a 30-minute hike on **Devastation Trail** through the cinder outfall before finally ending with a 0.8-mile hike to **Keanakāko'i Crater**.

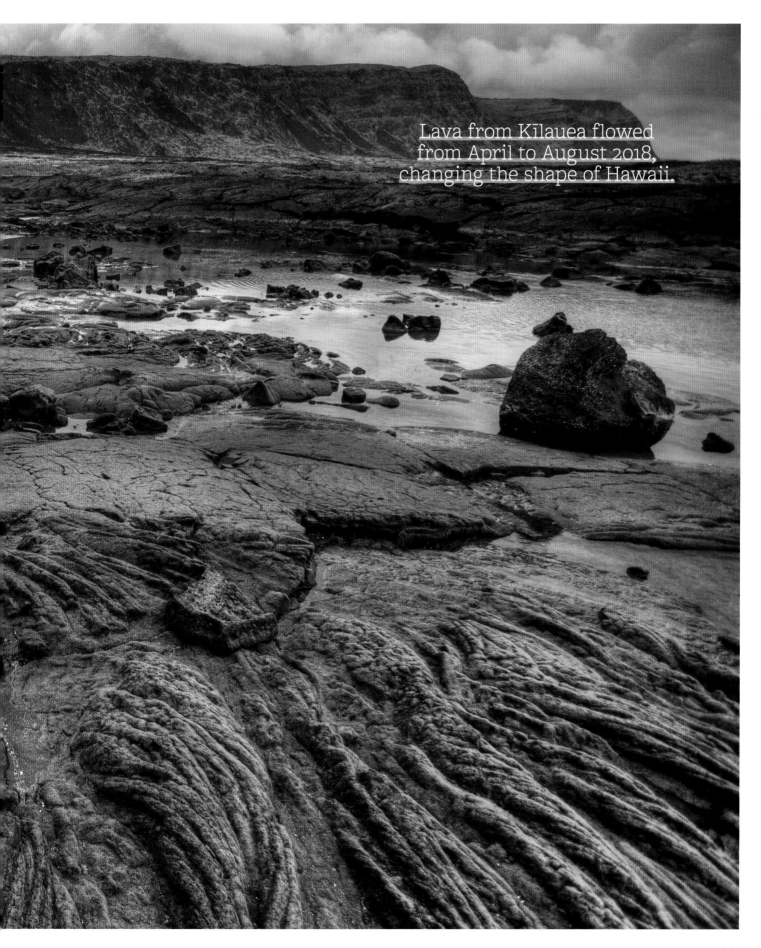

Lava from Kīlauea flowed
from April to August 2018,
changing the shape of Hawaii.

AMERICAN SAMOA

National Park of American Samoa

For a peek at the rocky coastal terrain and soothing blue waters, take the short 0.1-mile **Pula Island Trail** from the end of the paved road in **Vatia Village**. From the village, hike the 2.2-mile **Tuafanua Trail** up a path that ends with a few ladders and a rope climb—but opens up to a rocky beach with a Pola Island view. For a more historical take, the 1.7-mile **World War II Heritage Trail** (also with steep ladders and rope climbs) includes exhibits that saved Samoa from entering the war.

ENCOMPASSING PARTS OF three volcanic islands (Tutuila, Ta'ū and Ofu), most of this park in the South Pacific is rain forest—and 4,000 acres of it is underwater. Situated 2,600 miles southwest of Hawaii, the only way to get to this unspoiled haven from the United States is via a Hawaiian Airlines flight to Pago Pago International Airport on Tutuila Island, which only runs twice a week. From there, inter-island flights are available.

And with that comes the opportunity to explore one of the most untouched and remote parks on the planet. For nature fiends, there are rare animals among the 800 native fish and 200 coral species. Of the most notable are the flying foxes, also known as fruit bats. The combination of the equatorial climate and the relative youth of the ocean island also means a large variety of plant species.

But National Parks aren't just about plants and animals—they're also about preserving history and culture, and this one honors traditional Samoan culture at its best. For the most authentic experience, sign up for the Homestay Program. It's a chance to truly immerse yourself in the village life by living in a fale (Samoan home) with a family and participating in their daily activities, from mat-weaving to cutting the endemic Pandanus (laufala) leaves.

Whether you're staying awhile or passing through, be sure to respect the nightly sā prayers, which happen around dusk, and if you're asked to share the local pepper plant root drink, called ava, make sure you spill a few drops before raising your glass and saying "manuia."

Virgin Islands National Park

THE BULK OF the Caribbean island of St. John is the Virgin Islands National Park, a T-shaped area made up of 7,259 acres on land and another 5,650 acres underwater. Fittingly, the area is best known for its pristine white beaches jutting into Pantone-perfect turquoise oceans.

With 302 species of fish and 50 coral species, experience the park under its surface by scuba diving or snorkeling. In the shallow Mahalo Bay, green sea turtles are a common sight in the early morning and late afternoon. Keep your eyes peeled and you may also spot angelfish in the northeastern area and octopus in the cracks of the coral. Over on Waterlemon Cay, there are large cushion sea stars, while Brown Bay boasts more conch. Nicknamed a "boater's paradise," skimming the waters offers another way to take in the sea life.

Along with the natural beauty comes a complicated history. The region is a mix of indigenous Caribbean cultures that arrived 2,500 to 3,000 years ago and the Taino culture that came about 500 to 1,000 years ago, as well as European colonial settlers who landed in 1493, and African slaves who were forced to work on the island.

Ranger-led tours can provide more depth into the mix of culture and history. The Reef Bay Trail excursion (which includes a 40-minute boat ride) takes a look at the ruins of sugar plantations as well as ancient rock carvings, while the Friends of the Virgin Islands National Park holds seminars on diverse topics from the island's native bats to Caribbean movement and dance.

The **Francis Bay Trail** starts by the Francis Bay Sugar Factory and includes stops to view mangroves and Mary's Point Estate house, while **Lind Point Trails** goes from the visitor center to Honeymoon Bay. **Cinnamon Bay** is ideal for beachfront strolls or easily accessible snorkeling, thanks to its gentle slope, while the soft white sand of **Hawksnest Bay** has plenty of shade below the sea grapes that line the shore.

In 1956, Laurance Rockefeller
donated his land on the island
to the National Parks Service so
it would remain undeveloped.

Historic Sites

The wonderment of these landmarks is rooted in the stories they have to tell

Aleutian Islands World War II National Historic Area

UNALASKA, ALASKA

With 14 major islands and 55 smaller ones stretching in an arc separating the Bering Sea and the Pacific Ocean, the Aleutian Islands appear to be one of the most remote areas on Earth. It has been home to the Unangâx people for more than 8,000 years. The Japanese fought for the region during World War II and occupied Attu and Kiska islands in 1942, but eventually left the next year, following a violent battle. Since 1996, the area on Amaknak Island has been designated a National Historic Area, inviting visitors to learn about the history of the region and the army base at Fort Schwatka.

ALASKA

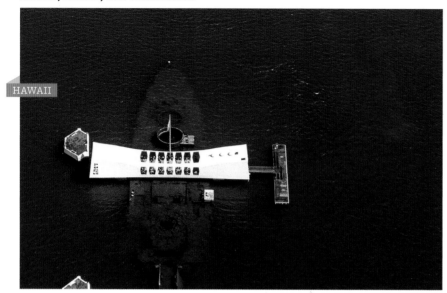

HAWAII

Pearl Harbor National Memorial

HONOLULU, HAWAII

On December 7, 1941, the Japanese bombed the *USS Arizona* battleship at Pearl Harbor, marking the United States' entrance into World War II. Today, an Alfred Preis–designed memorial—built in 1962—sits above the sunken ship, honoring the 1,177 sailors and Marines who were killed in the attack. The monument, located off Ford Island to the west of Honolulu, offers free 75-minute visits, including the boat ride and a film, but reservations for the timed tickets are recommended.

Last Command Post

SAIPAN, NORTHERN MARIANA ISLANDS

The little-known island of Saipan, part of the U.S. commonwealth of the Northern Mariana Islands (along with Tinian and Rota), is steeped in World War II American history, with a 113-acre American Memorial park dedicated to the 5,204 lives lost during the Invasion of Saipan. Just up the way is the Inos Peace Park, which opened in 2017. But it's the Last Command Post of Banadero, located below the Mapri Cliffs on the northern tip of the island, that leaves behind the most striking relics, including tanks and guns.

SAIPAN

VIRGIN ISLANDS

Fort Christian

CHARLOTTE AMALIE, U.S. VIRGIN ISLANDS

Built in 1680, Fort Christian—named after Danish King Christian V—is the oldest building to be used continuously on St. Thomas. Originally built as a fort, the structure has also been used as a police headquarters, governor's residence, a place of worship and now as a museum, which includes exhibits on the history of the Virgin Islands. A three-tiered tower serves as the centerpiece of the Gothic Revival–style building.

Castillo San Felipe del Morro

SAN JUAN, PUERTO RICO

Nicknamed El Morro, the six-floor fort at San Juan Bay has become symbolic of Old San Juan, especially with its notable round garitas, 60-foot walls and cannons. The foundations for the site were started in 1539 and completed in 1787 as one of the biggest Spanish fortifications in the Caribbean. Also part of the historic site is the adjacent Castillo San Cristóbal, which was built to further protect the city after attacks by the English and Dutch around the turn of the 16th century.

SPECIAL THANKS TO CONTRIBUTING WRITERS
RACHEL CHANG, VICKY HODGES, REBECCA KINNEAR, AUDREY ST. CLAIR

CENTENNIAL BOOKS

An Imprint of
Centennial Media, LLC
1111 Brickell Avenue, 10th Floor
Miami, FL 33131, U.S.A.

CENTENNIAL BOOKS is a trademark of Centennial Media, LLC

ISBN 978-1-955703-01-7

Distributed by
Simon & Schuster, Inc.
1230 Avenue of the Americas
New York, NY 10020, U.S.A.

For information about custom editions, special sales and premium and corporate purchases, please contact Centennial Media at contact@centennialmedia.com.

Manufactured in China

10 9 8 7 6 5 4 3

Publishers & Co-Founders Ben Harris, Sebastian Raatz
Editorial Director Annabel Vered
Creative Director Jessica Power
Executive Editor Janet Giovanelli
Features Editor Alyssa Shaffer
Deputy Editors Ron Kelly, Anne Marie O'Connor
Managing Editor Lisa Chambers
Design Director Martin Elfers
Senior Art Director Pino Impastato
Art Directors Jaclyn Loney, Natali Suasnavas, Joseph Ulatowski
Copy/Production Patty Carroll, Angela Taormina
Senior Photo Editor Jenny Veiga
Production Manager Paul Rodina
Production Assistant Alyssa Swiderski
Editorial Assistant Tiana Schippa
Sales & Marketing Jeremy Nurnberg